D1109405

Louis-Hippolyte LaFontaine and Robert Baldwin

ALSO IN THE
EXTRAORDINARY CANADIANS
SERIES:

SERIES EDITOR:
John Ralston Saul

Louis-Hippolyte LaFontaine and Robert Baldwin

by JOHN RALSTON SAUL
SERIES EDITOR

EXTRAORDINARY
CANADIANS

PENGUIN CANADA

Published by the Penguin Group

Penguin Group (Canada), 90 Eglinton Avenue East, Suite 700,
Toronto, Ontario, Canada M4P 2Y3 (a division of Pearson Canada Inc.)

Penguin Group (USA) Inc., 375 Hudson Street, New York, New York 10014, U.S.A.
Penguin Books Ltd, 80 Strand, London WC2R 0RL, England
Penguin Ireland, 25 St Stephen's Green, Dublin 2, Ireland (a division of Penguin Books Ltd)
Penguin Group (Australia), 250 Camberwell Road, Camberwell, Victoria 3124, Australia
(a division of Pearson Australia Group Pty Ltd)
Penguin Books India Pvt Ltd, 11 Community Centre, Panchsheel Park,
New Delhi – 110 017, India
Penguin Group (NZ), 67 Apollo Drive, Rosedale, North Shore 0745, Auckland, New Zealand
(a division of Pearson New Zealand Ltd)
Penguin Books (South Africa) (Pty) Ltd, 24 Sturdee Avenue, Rosebank,
Johannesburg 2196, South Africa

Penguin Books Ltd, Registered Offices: 80 Strand, London WC2R 0RL, England

First published 2010

1 2 3 4 5 6 7 8 9 10 (RRD)

Copyright © John Ralston Saul, 2010

Manufactured in the U.S.A.

LIBRARY AND ARCHIVES CANADA CATALOGUING IN PUBLICATION

Saul, John Ralston, 1947-
Louis Hippolyte LaFontaine and Robert Baldwin / John Ralston Saul.

(Extraordinary Canadians)
ISBN 978-0-670-06732-9

1. LaFontaine, L. H. (Louis Hippolyte), 1807-1864. 2. Baldwin, Robert, 1804-1858.
3. Prime ministers—Canada—Biography. 4. Canada—Politics and government—1841-1867.
5. Politicians—Canada—Biography. 6. Canada— History—1841-1867. I. Title.
II. Series: Extraordinary Canadians

FC470.A1S38 2010   971.04'2092   C2010-903064-8

Visit the Penguin Group (Canada) website at **www.penguin.ca**

Special and corporate bulk purchase rates available; please see
www.penguin.ca/corporatesales or call 1-800-810-3104, ext. 477 or 474

This book was printed on 30% PCW recycled paper

For Michael Cross, Eric Bédard, Robert Fraser
and Thomas Hodd,
four writers who have shown
how history sits waiting for us to open it up
and understand anew

CONTENTS

How do civilizations imagine themselves? One way is for each of us to look at ourselves through our society's most remarkable figures. I'm not talking about hero-worship or political iconography. That is a danger to be avoided at all costs. And yet people in every country do keep on going back to the most important people in their past.

This series of Extraordinary Canadians brings together rebels, reformers, martyrs, writers, painters, thinkers, political leaders. Why? What is it that makes them relevant to us so long after their deaths?

For one thing, their contributions are there before us, like the building blocks of our society. More important than that are their convictions and drive, their sense of what is right and wrong, their willingness to risk all, whether it be their lives, their reputations, or simply being wrong in public. Their ideas, their triumphs and failures, all of these somehow constitute a mirror of our society. We look at these people, all dead, and discover what we have been, but also what we can be. A mirror is an instrument for measuring ourselves. What we see can be both a warning and an encouragement.

These eighteen biographies of twenty key Canadians are centred on the meaning of each of their lives. Each of them is very different, but these are not randomly chosen great figures. Together they produce a grand sweep of the creation of modern Canada, from our first steps as a democracy in 1848 to our questioning of modernity late in the twentieth century.

All of them except one were highly visible on the cutting edge of their day while still in their twenties, thirties, and forties. They were young, driven, curious. An astonishing level of fresh energy surrounded them and still does. We in the twenty-first century talk endlessly of youth, but power today is often controlled by people who fear the sort of risks and innovations embraced by everyone in this series. A number of them were dead – hanged, infected on a battlefield, broken by their exertions – well before middle age. Others hung on into old age, often profoundly dissatisfied with themselves.

Each one of these people has changed you. In some cases you know this already. In others you will discover how through these portraits. They changed the way the world hears music, thinks of war, communicates. They changed how each of us sees what surrounds us, how minorities are treated, how we think of immigrants, how we look after each other, how we imagine ourselves through what are now our stories.

You will notice that many of them were people of the word. Not just the writers. Why? Because civilizations are built around many themes, but they require a shared public language. So Laurier, Bethune, Douglas, Riel, LaFontaine, McClung, Trudeau, Lévesque, Big Bear, even Carr and Gould, were masters of the power of language. Beaverbrook was one of the most powerful newspaper publishers of his day. Countries need action and laws and courage. But civilization is not a collection of prime ministers. Words, words, words – it is around these that civilizations create and imagine themselves.

The authors I have chosen for each subject are not the obvious experts. They are imaginative, questioning minds from among our leading writers and activists. They have, each one of them, a powerful connection to their subject. And in their own lives, each is engaged in building what Canada is now becoming.

That is why a documentary is being filmed about each subject. Images are yet another way to get at each subject and to understand their effect on us.

The one continuous, essential voice of biography since 1961 has been the *Dictionary of Canadian Biography*. But there has not been a project of book-length biographies such as Extraordinary Canadians in a hundred years, not since the Makers of Canada series. And yet every generation understands the past differently, and so sees in the mirror of these remarkable figures somewhat different lessons. As history rolls on, some truths remain the same while others are revealed in a new and unexpected way.

What strikes me again and again is just how dramatically ethical decisions figured in these people's lives. They form the backbone of history and memory. Some of them, Big Bear, for example, or Dumont, or even Lucy Maud Montgomery, thought of themselves as failures by the end of their lives. But the ethical cord that was strung taut through their work has now carried them on to a new meaning and even greater strength, long after their deaths.

Each of these stories is a revelation of the tough choices unusual people must make to find their way. And each of us as readers will find in the desperation of the Chinese revolution, the search for truth in fiction, the political and military dramas, different meanings that strike a personal chord. At first it is that personal emotive link to such figures which draws us in. Then we find they are a key that opens the whole society of their time to us. Then we realize that in that 150-year period many of them knew each other, were friends, opposed each other. Finally, when all these stories are put together, you will see that a whole new debate has been created around Canadian civilization and the shape of our continuous experiment.

That experiment in its modern form stretches back four hundred years to the original meeting of First Nations' civilizations with those of Europe. The most recent chapter, that of a democratic federation, is the subject of this series. It was structured and first put in place not in 1867, but between 1848 and 1851.

The Great Ministry, the government of LaFontaine and Baldwin, laid the foundations of Canada at its best. The idea of an inclusive society, of a citizenry that revels in social complexity, of a society in which personal restraint makes complexity a positive force, of above all a society devoted to fairness: all of this was formalized at the national level by LaFontaine and Baldwin.

The ongoing dramas of Canada – positive and negative – were shaped and energized as if in perpetuity by these two men and their great friendship.

Louis-Hippolyte LaFontaine and Robert Baldwin

CHAPTER ONE

Everything in One Moment

Monday, April 30, 1849

Two friends stood, as they often did, close together, quite still, occasionally exchanging quiet words inaudible to the others. In any case their words were muffled by the screams of rioters. It was early afternoon. A troop of professional infantry was holding the mob back, just out of sight at the top of Place Jacques-Cartier, only fifty metres down the street. The insults were easy enough to decipher. They were aimed at the two of them, Louis-Hippolyte LaFontaine, the prime minister, and Robert Baldwin, his closest ally.

They were standing in the small, pleasant courtyard of the old Château Ramezay in the centre of Montreal. For the last four years it had been Government House. With the Château behind them they could gaze over the low decorative wall of the courtyard, out across the Rue Notre-Dame, cleared of the mob only moments before, onto the formal gardens that stretched down to the city parade grounds, the Place d'Armes. All of this remains much as it was, except that the current City Hall was later built on the gardens.

There was a certain dissonance in the cries and taunts and threats of the mob, dominated by guttural northern Irish accents and the braying of the sons of the city's Protestant elite. Behind the two solitary leaders, officials were waiting, watching them. Others watched from the windows above. Watching for signs of panic, of emotional disarray. That is what the servants of power do when power is at risk. They watch for signs. Signs of firmness, of calm – in other words, of leadership – or of confusion or fear, signs of impending failure and the loss of power. The two friends knew that their role at that moment was to emanate absolute calm and self-confidence.

Every few minutes a policeman or a political informant would slip through the gates, brief the two men and disappear back out into the melee. The rioters had spread through the streets all around the Château, as many as five thousand of them, far more than the police and soldiers combined. Besides, the majority of the soldiers were local militia, a militia largely sympathetic to the mob. The government of Canada was surrounded and overwhelmingly outnumbered by rioters wanting to overthrow it. From Place Jacques-

Cartier and the Nelson Column they were thick all along Rue Notre-Dame and apparently armed, at the very least, with paving stones and eggs.

LaFontaine and Baldwin were waiting for the arrival of the Governor General, Lord Elgin. To reach Government House he would have to get through the mob. For protection he had with him a dozen local militia cavalry, again of uncertain loyalty.

It was just after two o'clock, Monday, April 30, 1849. Fourteen months before, following a surprisingly fair election and the defeat of the old pro–Family Compact government, Canada had become a democracy. It was the outcome of almost a decade of integrated work by francophone and anglophone Reformers, building a new political party around a program of hundreds of radical changes. On March 11, 1848, LaFontaine, francophone and Catholic, had become the first real prime minister of a democratic Canada. In Nova Scotia, a month earlier, on February 7, Joseph Howe and James Uniacke had accomplished the same thing "without a blow struck … or pane of glass broken," as Howe put it. But they were operating in far less complicated circumstances.

These successes in some ways were part of a democratic reform movement that was racing across Europe. It had begun with a revolution in January in Sicily. Then came the change in Nova Scotia in early February. A revolution in Paris followed later that month. Then Canada. Metternich, the architect of European conservatism after the fall of Napoleon, was driven from office in Vienna and went into exile in mid-March. In Berlin the army opened fire and nine hundred died, but the movement continued. The first Germany-wide pro-democracy parliament was in place by May. In Prague, in Budapest, in Transylvania, in Venice, Milan, Rome, and even in Vienna the emperors and princes and governors, even the Pope, fled or abdicated or gave up real power. A few of these leaders were killed. In Stockholm there were riots and deaths. In London, the twenty-nine-year-old Queen Victoria was advised by the government to withdraw with her husband and six small children to the Isle of Wight. The Bank of England was enveloped in sandbags with artillery behind them. Eighty-five thousand anti-reform citizens were sworn in as special constables. From January on, autocrat after autocrat had fallen or given in to the reformers' demands until virtually every government in Europe had been changed in favour of liberalism and democracy. The result was an unprecedented revolution throughout Western civilization.

And then, in June, just as abruptly as it had begun, the revolution began to collapse. Prague was bombarded. There was a counter-revolution. In Germany the princes struck back and the parliamentary movement dissolved. By October the imperial authorities had retaken Vienna. The Pope was soon back in Rome. France, after thousands of violent deaths, was slipping toward yet another imperial dictatorship. Democracy almost everywhere had been unseated and shoved back into a cell for many decades, in some cases until 1989. Tens of thousands had died.

We have always pretended that none of this was relevant to us in our little isolated colony, that somehow we didn't know what was going on elsewhere. Or that Canada was too unimportant, too colonial, too unsophisticated to be part of a major international intellectual and ethical movement.

But Europe's democratic spring was entirely relevant, even if the social and political model and the outcome here were the opposite of there. What happened here was intentionally different and therefore revealing of Canada's emergence as an atypical nation-state.

What was revolutionary in Canada was not so much the arrival of democracy as its conception. Democracy arrived as a broad program of social, political, economic and administrative policies consciously and intellectually designed to bring together opposing religions, languages and races. What was radical was the idea that a fair democracy could be based not on a definition of race as an expression of the nation state, but on what today we would call diversity; fairness was the key to diversity and diversity to fairness. The second revolutionary fact was that the Canadian movement was based on the rigorous use of political restraint, precisely the opposite of reform and revolutionary movements in Europe and the United States. Third, the reform movement here would manage to hold on to power while the others collapsed.

One technical reality lay at the core of what happened here. This was the first decade of the telegraph's use in Canada. News travelled back and forth between Montreal, Toronto, Halifax, New York, and the European capitals within a week to ten days. Curiously, word of the revolution in Paris had taken a few days longer and so arrived just after the March 11 democratic breakthrough in Montreal. But the point is that Europe's 1849 spring of hope was covered at great length in all the Canadian papers. Every detail was immediately served up and discussed by editorialists on all sides. And then from June on the reversals across the continent were reported in equal detail. The Western world was heading into an authoritarian era.

And the anti-democratic mobs in Montreal in April 1849 knew all of this. They believed in authoritarian and racially based government – in their particular case, of the Irish and Scottish Protestant sort. And they knew that everywhere else conservative authoritarianism was back, as was respect for class as the appropriate structure for power. They therefore saw themselves not as mobs but as the representatives of the triumphant wave of history.

LaFontaine and Baldwin themselves knew that they were on the losing side and that everywhere democrats had been defeated through exactly the sort of violence that had taken over the streets of Montreal that afternoon. The isolation of the prime minister and his friend in the courtyard of the Château Ramezay was symbolic of the isolation of democracy throughout the West.

Five days before, on April 25, Elgin had come to town to give formal assent to forty-two reform laws that Parliament had voted through. One of them – the Rebellion Losses Bill – had already become the focal point of the Opposition, which insisted it was an act of disloyalty, if not of treason. It would compensate innocent citizens who had lost property during the 1837 Rebellion. This had already been done for Upper Canadians. But they were British. The Opposition claimed that in Lower Canada the money would go to former rebels. After all, it would go to French Canadians, and in a stunning leap of logic, no French Canadian, by national or racial definition, was capable of real loyalty. Street demonstrators took up this theme of disloyalty and treason: parliamentary support for rebels amounted to governmental treason, which in turn justified violence by loyal citizens. There was, after all, an established British history of loyal citizens overthrowing disloyal governments. On the night of April 25 these self-defined loyalists turned into a mob, attacked the grand Parliament building, which stood on what is now the Place d'Youville at the other end of town from the Château Ramezay, and left it gutted by fire.

The next morning eighty or so distraught, confused, angry parliamentarians of all parties assembled in the new and equally grand Bonsecours Market, the long, high neo-classical building that still stands just around the corner from the Château. They were now even more deeply divid-ed by their rival beliefs of what constituted loyalty. The Assembly met upstairs in the unfinished, unheated, cav-ernous West Ballroom. They stood or sat hunched on a few rough benches. Three days later, on Saturday the twenty-eighth, they voted along party lines for or against an Address to the Governor General – a statement of admira-tion for his loyalty to Canadian democracy. Their Address was an assertion of words over violence, of debate over race and religion, but also of the public good over commercial power. The elected majority was not going to bow before the mob.

This optimistic document was ridden urgently out to the Governor General at his official residence – Monklands – several kilometres beyond the city limits, on the west side of Mont Royal. The house stands today almost as it was then, a vaguely Italian-style villa, now used as a girls' school. Lord Elgin agreed to come into town on Monday. He would come in full vice-regal regalia, in the state coach, pulled by two pairs of horses, led by a cavalry escort also in dress uniform, in order to have these words of democratic loyalty read to him with the full formality of the state in the presence of his government and his Parliament by the Speaker of the House. The whole exercise was an assertion that life in Montreal had returned to normal.

And so LaFontaine and Baldwin stood in the courtyard of the Château Ramezay on that cool spring Monday afternoon, waiting for him, as if in the dead space at the centre of a hurricane. You could think of them as a young but mature couple, having met in their mid-thirties and taken power in their mid-forties. A few exchanged words would be enough for mutual understanding. They were not talkative men, not orators, not tribunes, not easy in their manners in the eternal way of politicians. They were introverts driven into the public place by their ideas. They stood at the eye of this storm because of their beliefs. Both were tall, taller than most, imposing, almost pathologically calm. Until recently, the standard readings of Canadian history have rarely looked beyond their surface characteristics.

LaFontaine, with an imposing forehead, the whole head large and handsome in a classical way on big shoulders, had something of the well-dressed bull about him. On the surface a rock of physical and emotional stability, he was often thought to be arrogant and pompous. His attitudes were more probably the protective guise of a man in almost constant physical pain, as often bedridden as out in public. Through his twenties he had been physically strong, ambitious, self-confident. But his illnesses had undermined all of that and removed what little taste he had for the public side of public life. And although happily married, he continued to long for the children his wife could not conceive.

Baldwin in his twenties and early thirties had been a brooding, romantic figure, given to poetry and psychic uncertainty in the manner of Goethe's *Young Werther*. Like LaFontaine he had an imposing public solidity about him. In reality he remained profoundly romantic in the full early-nineteenth-century sense of that word. This inner life was carefully hidden from public view, even if the resulting outer calm came at great cost. He radiated the self-confidence of a man born into the elite and driven by his principles, but he was in permanent mourning, emotionally crippled by the death of his wife thirteen years before. She was his one passionate all-consuming love, dead at twenty-five, and he had never recovered. LaFontaine was among the few who understood this. That was one of the binding elements in their friendship, that and his attachment to Baldwin's children, the children he himself had not had.

We cannot know what they said to each other in undertones that afternoon as they waited and waited, standing like an immovable single force, emanating calm and restraint and intellectual argument and legal frameworks and stubbornness, as if all of their ethical and intellectual weaponry could will our fragile democracy to hold together.

We know even less what the Governor General and his brother, Colonel Bruce, were chatting about as they bumped along the quiet country road into town; perhaps about Elgin's new and sickly wife who was on the verge of giving birth to their first child. Elgin was a solid, almost cherub-like figure, ebullient, charming in both English and French. A natural politician. He would have had little hint of what lay ahead until the procession turned onto the west end of Rue Notre-Dame. The plump Major Jones, commanding the local militia cavalry escort – the Queen's Light Dragoons – would have seen the crowds filling the kilometre of street separating them from the Château Ramezay. The state coach had glass panes on the front and the sides, but the horses would have blocked the passenger's view forward. Jones would have ridden up to the window to report to Elgin. At first he would have been uncertain whether the crowd was friendly, unfriendly or mixed. After all, the government's supporters might have came out into the streets in reaction to the earlier riots staged by their enemies. Almost half the city was francophone and they would cheer, as would the large population of Irish Catholics. And there were, after all, also anglophone Protestant Reformers in Montreal.

The crowd thickened into thousands as the carriage advanced, then the rocks and eggs began flying. The windows were smashed. Both men were repeatedly hit. Jones kept his men in a tight cordon around the coach and tried to keep it moving as the mob closed in on them. Sitting inside a closed carriage you are in a cage – hardly protected, in full view, unable to do anything. Elgin sat as still as possible, blanched, moving only to avoid the stones, as their pace slowed almost to a halt and the verbal and physical filth rained in on them.

We know exactly what LaFontaine and Baldwin believed was at stake as they stood waiting. They constantly expressed their ideas and principles in speeches, articles and letters both political and personal. And yet the common interpretation built up over the past 160 years tends to ignore their ideas and to rush over these events, as if our stable, middle-class democracy didn't and doesn't want to think of itself as an intentional and controversial project and hates to be reminded of riots and a burning Parliament and anti-democratic fervour, all led by our established elites. There are no plaques or statues in Montreal explaining where, why, how we became a democracy, or how real and unusual choices were made. There is nothing displayed in the Château Ramezay or the Bonsecours Market. To know exactly where the Parliament stood, you must do archival research. Its walls are the outer perimeter of the surface parking lot on Place d'Youville!

And so we have ended up thinking that Canada stumbled into democracy. We still insist on the central importance of *our* common-law and civil-code origins, as if such British and French roots explain something essential. And yet the anti-democratic movement and the riots that day were led precisely by those who claimed they were loyal to the British way. And in France the civil-code tradition was at that very moment generously spilling blood and embracing an imperial dictatorship under Napoleon III.

Our standard historical interpretations skip quickly over the arrival in 1848 of an apparently technical concept – Responsible Government – then rush on to what are presented as the European-style triumphs and tragedies of the Canadian state. The few explanations given for the crisis of 1849 are concentrated on racial and religious tensions and financial interests, thus reinforcing the old European idea that people cannot help but be divided by race, religion, language and economic interests. The standard ways of understanding imply that no great or difficult intellectual or ethical or political choices were being advanced in Montreal that April.

The events of 1848 and 1849 are interpreted and measured through the lens of the European option of the monolithic nation-state, which is curious since the essence of the Canadian reform movement that came to power in 1848 was the idea of a bilingual state, built on immigration, multiple religions and regional differences. In other words, a non-monolithic, non-European model. Why, then, do we continue to see our history through the lens of the European-style nation-state, which failed disastrously, killing a hundred million of its own in the first half of the twentieth century alone? This rushing carelessly over our own events and our insistent dependence on European intellectual parameters continues to undermine our sense of why we are the way we are.

As I have argued in earlier books, there were already multiple and visible suggestions of what we might become in our long history, in our Aboriginal past and present, in the adoption of immigrants into the circles of our existing societies. The difference between what happened in Europe – including Britain – in 1848 and 1849 and what happened in Canada provides a road map to many of those ideas in play.

It is almost impossible today to feel the context of that time. Canada consisted of the southern part of Quebec and Ontario. It contained a society arguably more democratic than those of other Western countries – again including Britain – with, for example, a much broader franchise cutting across religious and racial lines. And beyond those borders and those of the other northern colonies lay Aboriginal societies democratic in a variety of ways that might almost be summarized as communitarian.

On the other hand, Canada's electoral politics were more violent than most, with club-wielding mobs fighting one another and massive corruption. It would be a mistake to think of its parliamentarians in contemporary terms. The Reformers may have belonged to a political movement devoted to restraint and non-violence, but in order to get to the hustings platforms to vote in their individual ridings, they had more often than not to fight their way through Orange Order mobs swinging clubs or armed gangs hired by the Family Compact government or the Governor General. Deaths were common.

LaFontaine and Baldwin had been formed as political thinkers and leaders by the failed uprisings of 1837 in Lower and Upper Canada. Without knowing the other, each had quickly come to almost identical conclusions: that the standard European, or indeed U.S., ideas of racial and class struggle could not work here. They didn't deny the importance of language and culture. To the contrary. They simply came to believe that the particular way of life in these northern territories meant that very different communities and individuals could be drawn together by ideas of the shared public good.

This was not self-evident. In the 1830s and 1840s no colony, perhaps ever in history, had extricated itself from the grip of an empire without fighting its way out or waiting for the empire to collapse. LaFontaine and Baldwin – and Howe, although he was more confused about the English link – developed an intellectual and political approach that was all about talking your way out, one argument at a time. It involved creating laws and programs that would make this evolution seem inevitable.

The violent reaction of their opponents in the spring of 1849 was in part designed to draw the reformers back into the mud – back into the supposed worldwide inevitability of violence based on racial, religious, linguistic differences. If they were successful, they believed, the empire would be obliged to intervene in order to stop the colonial mobs from killing one another. Power would then revert to the group loyal to the imperial authorities.

And so the first characteristic of the LaFontaine–Baldwin philosophy was a devotion to restraint. In the violent context of the time this would be mistaken for weakness and indecision. Power was a metaphor for the constant maintenance of order. If this required violence, so be it. A government's job was to disperse mobs, if necessary by opening fire. In 1849 in Montreal the local anglophone-dominated militia were probably not to be trusted to do that. But there were more than enough British regulars to do a professional job. Properly lined up, opening fire in raking blasts, they could disperse mobs many times their own size. That, after all, is how empires are held. The soldiers are always outnumbered by the locals. That's why, when they open fire, their intent is to achieve a mass effect by killing large numbers. The Canadian government's refusal to keep order by shooting the mob, in fact their refusal to keep order at all, was considered a failure of weakness by London, by the mob itself, even by much of the Reform elite.

Restraint was such a new and audacious strategy that its power was not at first self-evident. The rioting had begun on the night of April 25, and for five days and nights LaFontaine and Baldwin hardly left Government House. The cabinet operated from there. When the capital had been moved to Montreal in 1844, a four-storey building was constructed behind the Château to hold government departments. LaFontaine, his wife and Baldwin discreetly moved into hotels near the Château Ramezay, but the two men scarcely had time to use their beds.

They armed loyal civilians, disarmed them a day later, arrested troublemakers, released them, negotiated with selected Opposition leaders, calmed their own MPs. Cabinet meetings ran all night. There were reports, proclamations, a press campaign in Montreal, a press campaign across the two Canadas. There was urgent correspondence about local militia with military rifles who might attempt a coup. Government leaders were attacked in the streets, their houses damaged. LaFontaine's new and handsome house was sacked. When attacked coming out of the temporary Parliament, he was rescued by soldiers. The details of managing disorder almost always look and feel like confusion at the time, and this was no exception. But the underlying line was that of restraint.

The combination of restraint and talking your way out of an empire would later become the method used in Australia and New Zealand, then in India and eventually in the early 1960s in colony after colony, in much of the British Empire and part of the French. But in 1849 in an atmosphere of violence and disorder it seemed an improbable strategy, constantly provoking accusations, in the language of the day, of unmanly behaviour.

But the dominant accusation was that of disloyalty. When you read the astonishing two-week debate over the Rebellion Losses Bill, you are caught off guard by the eloquence, the anger, the intellectual sophistication, the verbal violence on both sides. What cannot be missed is that this was a struggle over the notion of loyalty. Everything turned on this eternal concept. Who was loyal, who a traitor? The leader of the Opposition, Sir Allan MacNab, and his allies had built their careers on the idea of loyalty to Queen, empire, race, religion, language. The assumption was that francophones were the adversaries and would therefore assert their own set of loyalties. And indeed there was a small, growing group of francophone nationalists who thought exactly that way. Thus both sides would be perfectly in line with what was unfolding in Europe, and in the United States, where a newly virulent nationalism had brought James Polk to the presidency under the slogan "Fifty-four Forty or Fight," the latitude representing the northern border of what was then the Oregon Territory, jointly occupied by the U.S. and Britain. The objective was that the United States should invade Canada to eject the British from the Territory. A loyal Canadian was therefore someone who was ready to fight back against any disloyalties – whether coming from Catholics or Americans, or even the occasional Protestant. Today this notion may ring hollow and seem ridiculous. Then it was the truth of Western civilization.

LaFontaine and Baldwin, and their allies – Francis Hincks, William Blake, Wolfred Nelson first among them – were arguing something new, something quite different: their opponents' loyalty was deeply treasonous because it sought to set citizens one against the other, religion against religion, language against language, race against race. True loyalty, the Reformers argued, was to the public good and to an ethically based well-being that brought people together.

At key historic moments every society burns into its unconscious the outline of patterns for agreement and disagreement. These become the civilizational model and remain in place for centuries. The spring of 1849 was the defining moment for modern Canada. On one side was the European monolithic model, the colonial party, loyal to whatever empire was dominant, provided that this loyalty brought them power, income and psychic comfort – power and income without real responsibility. Like all colonial elites they were pessimistic about their own capacity as elites to think and act in a manner appropriate to this place. On the other side was a democratic movement that sought to develop new approaches to the public good. In Canada that meant loyalty to an unprecedented idea of complexity, which in turn meant that everyone, leaders in particular, would have to discipline themselves through restraint – restraint as encouragement to a civilization of complexity involving *the other*. Each Canadian crisis since 1849 has been a replay of these opposing patterns.

On that April afternoon the prime minister and his friend could not know most of this. But they knew they were in uncharted territory. And they knew that reformers throughout the West had been destroyed by acting and reacting in a predictable manner. Salvation lay in the unpredictable.

IT WAS TWENTY AFTER TWO. A police officer ran in to tell them that the state coach had appeared at the far end of Rue Notre-Dame, a few minutes later that the mob was surging about it. Somewhere out of sight the highly experienced but rather ancient Lieutenant-General Sir Benjamin d'Urban, the senior military officer in the Canadas, was attempting to use his soldiers to ease the situation. He had agreed to the government policy that his troops would not open fire on the mob. The strain on d'Urban was so great that he collapsed and died a few weeks later.

LaFontaine and Baldwin could not help wondering if they hadn't miscalculated by bringing the Governor General into town. If he were killed or wounded, the mob would have defeated itself. The empire could never side with a party that killed its representative. But it would be a pyrrhic victory for the Reformers. The dye of violence and division would have been set. Their philosophy of restraint would also have been proved unworkable.

They could hear the mob degenerating into violence. Word came that Elgin was surrounded, blocked, effectively their hostage. Then Major Jones and his cavalry whipped up their horses and the carriage came bursting through, swerving into the courtyard half wrecked. Elgin emerged from his filthy, broken-in cage carrying a large stone and disappeared inside the Château. He had lost his cocked hat. His uniform was a mess. The two friends gave orders that the parliamentarians should now be brought over from the Bonsecours

Market to present their Address, then followed the Governor General inside.

From the market to the Château is a pleasant two-minute stroll when there isn't a mob blocking the way. The Opposition boycotted the ceremony, but fifty MPs – virtually the whole Reform caucus – led by the Speaker of the House, came down the wooden stairs from the ballroom and out under the hoarding of the uncompleted facade into the melee on Rue Saint-Paul. A regiment of regular soldiers created a protective ring around the MPs and attempted to push their way across Saint-Paul into the maelstrom of Rue Saint-Claude, the narrow street leading up to the Château. Stones, eggs, rotten vegetables rained down on them. At one point the infantry charged with bayonets fixed and the mob fell back.

In any case these parliamentarians were a tough group. Dr. Wolfred Nelson and the young George-Étienne Cartier were among them, leaders at the Battle of Saint-Denis in 1837 when they had defeated a British force of regulars; Francis Hincks had created a gang of Montreal Irish Catholics for election riots; the solicitor general, William Blake, had taken to carrying a pistol.

We are often told that liberal intellectuals are soft, cut off in the world of ideas, while men of action – physical action –

tend to be anti-intellectual and on the right. This government, which created the foundations of modern Canada,
was led by intellectuals formed in physical action. It was all
the more remarkable that their aim was to change the system
in order to remove the violence. But if the soldiers couldn't
protect them, they were probably capable of fighting their
own way through the mob.

They eventually arrived in the courtyard of the Château
Ramezay in the same filthy state as Elgin. The Address was
duly read out: "We have witnessed with feelings of deep sor-
row … a mob of rioters … in a time of profound peace and
tranquility have committed … wanton and disgraceful out-
rages…. We further beg leave to express … our deep sense of
the justice and impartiality which has uniformly character-
ized the constitutional government of Your Excellency…."

Elgin replied, "A free people can hardly fail to discover, in
the faithful observance of all constitutional narratives, the
best security for the preservation of their rights and liberties."

Then the MPs melted away and the cabinet sat down to
a long strategy session, while fighting spread through the
streets and barricades went up on Rue Notre-Dame to
block the Governor General's departure. Elgin had to be
extricated without a battle, so they slipped him out the east
side of the courtyard, his carriage cutting along Rue

Gosford, to Rue Saint-Denis and up to Sherbrooke. The mob got wind of his escape and dashed in their carriages and on horseback to cut him off at Sherbrooke and Saint-Laurent. They were, after all, the elite. They had carriages and horses. Now they began stoning him in earnest, and the carriage was broken in on all sides. His brother was badly wounded on the head. They escaped again by breaking off on a track to the right and going all the way around the back of the mountain. When Elgin arrived home he picked up two sharp cobblestones from the floor of his state carriage as presents for his pregnant wife. She wrote a label for each stone and glued them on, then had a box built for storage. He remained at Monklands for four months under military protection while things cooled off and the government governed. The box with the labelled rocks can be seen today in Ottawa in the National Archives. He would later use the same carriage for state openings of Parliament, its outside panels unrepaired, to remind the elite of how badly they had acted.

It would be several hours before LaFontaine and Baldwin knew that he had successfully escaped.

CHAPTER TWO

A Romantic Youth

To be born the eldest male of a rich and powerful man is a present to no child. Worse still, if your father has a personality both overwhelming and engaging and devotes himself to public causes. What space remains for the child? Robert Baldwin struggled with this burden all his life. At no point did he lack for anything that money could buy. At no moment did he lack for love, fatherly adoration and maternal support. Fortunately, his father had that rare talent among powerful men: he knew how to build up his son, not destroy him.

William Warren Baldwin believed passionately in family. He believed in the creation of a dynasty, from eldest son to eldest son, establishing their place in society while doing good along the way. He was a Whig in the full British sense – an aristocrat imbued with noblesse oblige: look after your interests, limit authority, seek some level of shared justice. In many ways he represented the best of that Whig tradition. And his son dutifully set out to fulfil his father's dream. Three events would throw him off that path and onto one of remarkable political originality. Put another way, Robert Baldwin's life began in the certainty of imported political concepts. These concepts and his certainty were smashed by Canadian realities. He then set about creating a new model, one generated both independently and together with Louis-Hippolyte LaFontaine.

The Baldwins arrived in Upper Canada in 1799. Robert Baldwin's grandfather, also called Robert, came out of the Irish ascendency, the Anglican Irish who held their place of power in Ireland because of English dominance. The Baldwins were not grand. They were landed gentry from county Cork and had commercial interests. The elder Robert Baldwin was a romantic. He was active in the Irish democratic reform movement, ran a pro-democracy publication, lost his money, went deeply into debt and was bailed out by his relatives. All of this, combined with the death of his wife, made him decide to immigrate to Canada, taking six of his many children with him. He was fifty-seven – old for such a radical decision. The children included four daughters, one as young as seven, and two sons, the eldest twenty-three. That was William Warren, a practising doctor, trained at the University of Edinburgh.

Their first ship failed at sea. The second left with their belongings but without them. They raced in a smaller boat to catch it. Their captain, a secret Bonapartist, almost sailed them into French hands. They were robbed, then recovered everything. In early summer 1799 they arrived in New York and made their way up the Hudson and Mohawk rivers on "schooners, sloops and bateaux," as William Warren put it. On these small, slow boats they baked under the sun and were eaten alive by mosquitoes. After several weeks they reached Oswego, on the south shore of Lake Ontario, and crossed over to the outer shore of what we now call Toronto Island, then a "carrying place of the Indians."

On the other side of this great sandbar lay a remarkable natural harbour, Toronto Bay, several kilometres long and a kilometre and a half wide. This harbour, the abundance of fresh water coming down small rivers and streams, along with the distance from the U.S. border, was why the site had been chosen by Governor Simcoe in 1793 as Upper Canada's capital. The Mississauga had been there forever. As so often in Canada's immigrant story, cities were placed exactly where First Nations lived or met and for precisely the same reasons worked out by those indigenous peoples. And so the Baldwins were rowed across the bay to York, where over the next six decades they would play a central role in the creation of a new kind of democracy.

The capital was a tiny village with neither churches nor schools, no inn, one store, a handful of houses spread mainly along the shore of the bay – Front Street – near the mouth of the Don River. The minute nature of the capital was a reminder that most of modern Ontario was then the world of the First Nations and the Métis. And even within the small southern world of Loyalist Upper Canada the few hundred people in York need to be weighed against the thousands of farmers and the six thousand First Nations Loyalists who had come to Niagara fifteen years before. What's more, the vast majority of Loyalists living outside York were neither English nor Anglican. Forty percent were from German religious minorities. Then there were the Aboriginals, the Irish and Scottish Catholics, the Black Loyalists.

York became Toronto, and its population would swell to thirty thousand by the time of the democratic revolution of mid-century. But even then the half million farmers living outside the cities would be the continuing force behind democratic reform.

York was therefore a strange world led by a small group of Anglicans, many of whom dreamed of creating a little England on the Tory model, with themselves as the beneficiaries. This colonial autocracy, which came to be known as the Family Compact, was already in place and gathering fresh supporters. As was its opposition, the nascent reform movement. John Beverley Robinson, John Strachan, Allan MacNab, the Boultons, the Jarvises would lead the Compact side against John Rolph, Marshall Bidwell, Jesse Ketchum, and of course William Lyon Mackenzie. For decades they would argue, plot, shoot at each other, flee into exile, be jailed and begin again.

The Baldwins arrived just before the struggle began. People were still busy building their fortunes, their place, their city. They didn't have much time for overt politics.

Within three decades they would turn Toronto into a fast-growing neoclassical city of avenues – even if the roads were dirt – grand public buildings, large houses, well-maintained wood sidewalks. It was only in the later nineteenth century that the neoclassical architecture with all its references to the British idea of Italy, Rome and Greece disappeared – lost in fires or pulled down in favour of the unfortunate dark, red-brick Victorian look brought in from Northern Ireland.

Robert Baldwin the elder arrived with two introductions to other immigrants from Cork – the senior figure in the colony, Peter Russell, and a businessman, William Willcocks. They were large landholders, and through marriage the Baldwins would end up inheriting and consolidating it all.

But first Robert showed his strange romantic character by buying a thousand acres on the shore of Lake Ontario, two days' sailing to the east. It lay around a beautiful inlet – his own natural harbour – just beyond where Oshawa now sits, almost in the shadow of the Darlington nuclear plant. He dragged his six children there to live the life of settlers, crowded into a small log cabin, clearing land, trying to make a living in a way for which he was too old and in which none of his family had any experience. He was an educated man and so was quickly named the local magistrate, the militia colonel, the county lieutenant – that is, the senior man in the area. And they cleared more land, planted orchards, lived a life both bucolic and back-breaking.

William Warren must have known all along that this could not be his real life. He went back and forth between their farm in Baldwin's Creek and the town of York, sailing a little boat or canoeing, often in risky weather. In 1801 he moved to York to practise as a doctor and live the life of a young bachelor – drinking with friends, sailing along the coast in mixed parties to picnic in picturesque spots like the mouth of the Humber, sailing with friends to his father's farm to hunt, fish and help with the harvest.

There weren't enough patients, so in 1802 he opened a school for young boys. A year later he became a lawyer and divided his life into doctoring, lawyering and teaching. That same year he married William Willcocks's daughter, Phoebe. He would always be devoted to her, and she would hold the family together as he rushed ahead in multiple directions. It was a happy if conventional marriage. A year later, May 12, 1804, Robert Baldwin was born at home on the northwest corner of Frederick and what is now Front Street. They would have four more boys; three would die in childhood or as teenagers. A few years later they would move to the northeast corner of Bay and Front, with a wonderful view across Toronto Bay. And then William Warren would build a large country house up on the ridge of the old shore of the prehistoric Lake Algonquin. He called it Spadina – a Native name for "up on the hill" – and around it created a great estate linking together family members.

To say that he built Spadina House should be taken literally. William Warren had now also become an architect, a planner and a developer. He set about building friends' Georgian mansions and competing for contracts on public buildings. One of the last memories of neoclassical Toronto is his – the elegant eastern wing of Osgoode Hall – still the seat of the Law Society of Upper Canada and virtually unchanged inside.

Below Spadina House he laid out a great tree-lined way to the inland sea. "I have cut an avenue through the woods all the way so that we can see the vessels passing up and down." This Spadina Avenue would later become the centre of immigrant Toronto.

Robert Baldwin's life would revolve around these two properties – one up on the shore of the old lake, the other down on the shore of the new – as would the creation of much of Canada as we know it.

It is hard not to see his childhood as idyllic. In the summers they sailed down the coast to their grandfather's farm, where they would live out what is still the classic dream of a Canadian summer, fishing, exploring, canoeing and helping in the fields. In the winter they walked out through their front door, crossed Front Street and skated on the bay. Later William Warren moved the family up to Spadina for the health of country living, and their spare time was spent in the gardens and forest around the house. Or they walked the five kilometres down into town and back up.

Robert's education, whether in his father's school or later in that of John Strachan, the conservative Anglican priest who would become the archangel of the Family Compact, was of the classical sort. But it was taught in an atmosphere of pleasure and excitement. Yes, he learnt what you might expect, a great deal of the Greeks and Romans. And yes, he became head boy at age fifteen and could be heard in a public examination

arguing in Latin. What is notable is the quality of the education and the inculcation of a love of reading. And he lived in a
family that discussed authors and ideas. The correspondence
much later between LaFontaine and Baldwin is filled with references to the purchase of books for each other. There is a hint
of the place he gave ideas in his highly emotional will of 1840.
Abruptly in the middle of regrets over his lost wife and the division of land, he pauses to leave to his cousin "Robert Baldwin
Sullivan my edition of Montesquieu's spirit of hero's in pur-
suance of a promise made to him many years since." (Here was
a further sign of his distraught state, as the title should have
been *The Spirit of the Laws*.)

WHEN THE WAR OF 1812 broke out, Robert was eight. By that
time his grandfather had given up the farm and moved to
town into their house. There was, as so often before wars
actually get under way, great enthusiasm for a fight. Phoebe
Baldwin led the ruling-class women, designing a flag for the
local militia. Strachan provided the motto. John Beverley
Robinson entertained the sewing ladies with poetry readings. General Isaac Brock dropped in to encourage the flag
makers. The Family Compact appeared to be seamless.

On April 27, 1813, a U.S. fleet of fourteen ships carrying
several thousand soldiers appeared suddenly from across the

lake and occupied Toronto Bay. The men of York rushed to join their militia regiments. William Warren was needed as a doctor. But they were an ill-organized force of a mere hundred who had to support a few companies of British regulars. It was the Mississauga and other Ojibwa who first found the invading troops not far from where they had landed and began a guerrilla-style defence. Uneven though the two sides were, the battle would last six hours.

The surprise of the attack had been so great that the fighting had begun before the women with their children and invalids could flee the town for safety. The Baldwins walked as fast as they could north up Yonge Street, a corduroy road – rough logs laid against each other – which meant they would have to make their way along the edges. They were three women, plus Robert and his younger brothers, two invalids, including Robert Baldwin the elder, as well as a carriage weighed down with food and clothes. Phoebe was in charge.

They had walked three kilometres when there was a great explosion, creating general panic among the refugees. The military gunpowder magazine near the garrison had blown up, sending its thick rock walls hurtling through the air like shrapnel. This event accounted for most of the American dead. William Warren was on the battlefield treating the wounded but was somehow untouched. Phoebe pulled her little group together, and they walked on several more kilo-metres through the woods to the small isolated farmhouse of Baron de Hoen, an immigrant French aristocrat with whom they were friends. He lived near today's Eglinton Avenue.

By the end of the day York had been occupied, looted and burnt. It was a disaster for the Canadians, but also for the Americans. No one could argue that here were the republican, honourable citizen soldiers of a great democracy. They had set in emotional stone for another century the resolve of the Canadians to resist any attempts at absorption. In the confu-sion people's reputations were made and broken. William Warren out on the battlefield treating the wounded of both sides showed that he was much more than an amusing, ambitious newcomer. John Strachan, bullying the American commander into getting control of his disorderly soldiers, showed that he was much more than an ambitious manipula-tor of religious doctrine. All of this became part of the Canadian myth that later merged with the crucial victory of Queenston Heights, Laura Secord's courageous trek through the snow to warn the British, Charles de Salaberry's remark-able victory in 1812 and his defence of Montreal in 1813.

But beneath this facade of unity and the immediate deifi-cation of General Brock as the heroic martyr after his death at Queenston, there were other forces at play. The British had failed the colonials at York. In battle after battle, the First Nations and the militia had played key roles, which gave each group fresh self-confidence. In addition, fundamental divisions were exposed. Brock, for example, had used the war to try to force the legislature to give up much of the little power it had. He was a general and he wanted a simpler, more authoritarian regime, including the limitation of habeas corpus. He had been blocked by a solid opposition – Whigs who believed that it was their duty to limit the power of authority. He tried dissolving the legislature and calling a wartime election, usually a sure bet for the reinforcement of authority, but even then was faced by a small, effective pro-democracy opposition able to slow him down. So he prorogued the Assembly to shut it up.

If you look dispassionately at the post-1815 mythologies you begin to notice that Brock and British domination became the rallying cry of loyalty on the Family Compact side. The heroism of John Strachan, the future bishop, of Allan MacNab, the future knight and leader of the Compact, of Lieutenant Fitzgibbon, to whom Laura Secord had carried her message – all of this was merged with military and religious nationalism as if it justified the right of a few families to control the colony. Well into the 1840s it was Sir Allan MacNab, now also the Compact's hero of 1837, who took on raising the funds to rebuild Brock's monument in Queenston Heights after it was blown up by the Fenians, the Irish nationalists whose North American faction sought to challenge British presence in the Canadas. And while the reformers or democrats were no fans of the Fenians, they didn't lift a finger to help fund the rebuilding of the monumental column. It was a symbol of colonial subjugation.

There was one other factor in play. All of this Britishness required the erasing of contradictory mythologies, for example that of the essential role of the First Nations in battles such as Queenston Heights. Against this colonialism a new democratic nationalism was emerging, and the hero of the democrats was the Shawnee martyr Tecumseh. He had won several battles, held the southern front and was killed after being abandoned on the field by the British regulars at the Battle of Moraviantown.

Robert Baldwin was a bad poet, but a persistent one. His two most interesting attempts, at fifteen years of age, four years after the war, are in praise of Tecumseh and therefore contemptuous of the British.

> Wrapt in the darkness of his soul he stands
> And casts a last indignant glance
> Upon the scattered British ...

Unlike the professional soldiers from Britain, the indigenous leader was

Resolved to perish rather than yield.

Tecumseh would not, could not, yield because this was his place. The message of the reformers was the same. Canada was, as Robert would later put it with satisfaction on returning from his one trip to England and Ireland, "my own, my native land." The reformers were showing signs of slipping free of the Whig idea of justice, but had not yet found another.

From his eighth to his eleventh year, Robert lived in or near a city twice occupied and burnt, as well as once unsuccessfully attacked. Those around him were equally marked. His father had been deeply disturbed by what he saw of war. His mother had come back into town just in time to drive off looters from their house, by force of personality alone. Even when the children were sent to live in safety on a farm, almost thirty kilometres from York, their lives were consumed by this drama. These were the defining years of Robert's youth, years that marked the way he imagined his own existence in this place.

IN 1820, AGED SIXTEEN, he went from Strachan's school to his father's law office as a clerk and set about learning the business. In that same year his younger brother Henry died, and his father threw himself into politics.

The Baldwins had every reason to veer to the right and blend into the Family Compact. Instead, they turned increasingly toward what passed for the left. In their family it seemed as if every personal tragedy pushed them further into the cause of public justice, as if the tragedies hardened the survivors' ethical edge and reduced the expectations they might have from family interests and triumphs. William Warren began speaking out against the corrupt legal system, the corrupt land transfer system, the unjustified power of the Church to which he belonged. He became the respectable face of the reform movement, was soon elected to the legislature and worked closely with Marshall Bidwell and John Rolph, both lawyers, the latter also a doctor. And whatever the three of them felt personally, they were also allied to the reform journalist William Lyon Mackenzie, with his strange, badly fitted wigs and his intemperate ways. More than anyone else Mackenzie spoke to the farmers and labourers and spoke for them.

Within a few years Robert would be working on major public, essentially political, cases with John Rolph. But politics would draw him in slowly. Far more important, his psychic energy was devoted to an obsessive search for love and the ideal woman. At first you might mistake this for the obsession of any young man, yet what emerged was quite different in its intensity. He wrote insistently to a close friend about the possibility that passion and love could be brought together between a man and a woman and that he could find that woman. As the historians Michael Cross and Robert Fraser have pointed out, he was a man who could open himself only to a woman. He therefore needed to find her for his own well-being.

Most descriptions of Robert are of a sickly, melancholy man, awkward in public. Most of these characteristics were based on recollections of his last, broken years. Descriptions of the younger man reveal someone who loved to dance, loved the jostle of family life, loved to have as many of his relatives as possible all living in his house. A friend put together a small volume of Baldwin's poetry. It includes twenty poems to women, most to individual women, not idealized abstractions. Images of the young man show a romantic. There is melancholy, but it is very much, as I have said, in the manner of Young Werther's sorrows.

At twenty-one he found her. She was fifteen and a first cousin. Elizabeth Sullivan. Eliza. They were overwhelmed by each other. And both families, horrified by her age and their close blood relationship, sent her away to New York. The sudden unexpected need to love by correspondence forced them to bring out their feelings and work out what they meant.

At first there was a raft of poems. May 14, 1825:

> The loved companion of my way
> My hope – my joy – my more than pride
> My beacon to a happier day –

May 15: "I threw myself into the chair that stands opposite the window and gave myself up to the most exquisitely painful train of reflections – the window was open and the perfume of the blossoms of the fruit trees and the buds of the Lylacks just opposite the window was blown in by the breeze – those were the very lylacks from which I used formerly to pluck bouquets for you."

Waiting for a letter from her, he hurried out of his family's sight, "again to the passage for I felt the tears rushing to my eye – I am a strange being, Eliza – I frequently bear pain without a tear – but joy always overcomes me."

This went on for two years. On the first day of each month at the same time in the evening they would meet in their spirits, thinking each about the other, talking to each other. "Ideal" meetings, he called them. He would look up into the sky "indulging in a thousand delightful recollections and anticipations."

In the midst of this extended personal drama he was called to the bar and began his work with John Rolph. Yet he confessed to Eliza that when he rose to speak in the courts he could think only of her.

Finally in 1827 she was allowed back and almost imme-diately they were married, she seventeen, he twenty-three. They moved at first into Spadina House. Nine years of obsessive happiness followed. They felt they had a perfect union, emotional, physical, intellectual. Robert later described this as "the most perfect and unbounded mutual confidence and affection." The key word here is *unbounded*. Everything else in his life had the boundaries of family, class, public obligation, ethical obligation.

He had confessed early on to Eliza his fear of failure. "I have a horror of not rising above mediocrity – I am not however by any means so certain of my future success as others seem to be." First among the others must have been his father. Robert's perfect love outside the restrictions of other's expectations gave him the confidence that he was more than their extension. He was his own expectation, or rather the expectation of two people's love. This was the first of the three seismic events that turned him into a great man.

His public confidence grew. His intelligence, combined with his ethical clarity, turned him into a dangerously effective attorney. He had a talent for solid, broad public argument that signalled to others, like Rolph and Bidwell, that he could become a spokesman for the reform movement. The whispering, halting manner of his speeches was so different from the booming style of the time that audiences went eerily silent in order to follow the arguments they had come to respect, even when they rejected them.

The nature of the battle before him was clear. In the year of Robert's marriage, John Strachan had pulled off a complex, secret negotiation in England giving 226,000 valuable – often urban – acres to the Anglican Church, as if it were the official state church of Upper Canada. This provided him with a rich and perpetual source of money – a political treasure chest. The resulting crisis became known as the Clergy Reserve problem and would last twenty-seven years.

Through the 1820s and 1830s the reformers fought and won a series of other battles. In 1829 an immigration bill was adopted that made Canadian nationals of those who had come earlier from the United States, not just from Britain.

This was the legal beginning of formalized Canadian citizenship, more than a century before the 1947 Citizenship Act, which was more the tying-up of a last loose thread than something new or revolutionary.

They held ever more public meetings calling for reforms in every direction. On August 15, 1828, William Warren chaired a large meeting at which Robert moved a resolution asserting that the constitution was a treaty between Britain and Canada; it would therefore require the assent of both parties to change it.

In the same year Robert ran for a parliamentary seat. His campaign was inept and he was defeated. He tried again the next year in a by-election, won and declared himself "a Whig in principle." He was right because the political battles of the first four decades of the century would be organized around imported ideas. You were a Whig or a Tory. You were against or for authoritarianism and financial self-interest – that is, corruption. There was another election in 1830. Robert lost and simply walked away, back to his intensely happy family life and his growing practice.

In 1835 Spadina House burnt down. William Warren rebuilt it immediately, but in a more modest way, and made it his home. He replaced the building at Front and Bay with a large, elegant neoclassical brick house, three storeys with a semi-basement for kitchens, five windows across, a big courtyard and coach house behind, gardens and orchards on two sides. This became Robert and Eliza's house and the centre of family life. It was probably the finest house in Toronto.

Two blocks to the west, also looking out over the bay, was John Strachan's big house, called "The Palace," even though he would not become Upper Canada's first Anglican bishop until 1839. Perhaps because he had married into a prominent merchant family – the McGills – he had been able to build his palace when he was a mere priest.

And one block farther to the west was the new Parliament, completed in 1832. It stood exactly on the footprint of today's CBC headquarters. It was also a neoclassical monument, stretched comfortably across the middle of three hectares of garden and also looking out over the bay. Behind it, where Roy Thomson Hall now stands, was the governor's residence, attached to the Parliament by its own large gardens. Each time a Baldwin walked out under his classical, columned porch and turned right to walk three blocks to Parliament, he would have to pass only one house – that of the spiritual leader of every idea and interest they opposed. Strachan was, as William Warren wrote to his son Robert in 1829, one of the governor's "evil advisers," along with John Beverley Robinson and a few others. This Parliament building would serve until the 1890s, when the by-then provincial legislature moved to Queen's Park. Some of the most important debates and decisions in the shaping of Canada took place there, which is why I suppose there is no sign indicating that it ever existed.

At the end of her fourth pregnancy, in April 1834, Eliza gave birth by Caesarean. She hemorrhaged. The doctor managed to save her. Infection followed, more hemorrhaging; it dragged on and on, month after month. Eliza's agony shredded Robert's soul. Their souls entwined. In the midst of her suffering he scribbled a note to his brother-in-law, Lawrence Heydon:

> Eliza Continues
> thank God rather better
> certainly not worse
> > God bless you
> > Robert
> > Tuesday 2 o'clock PM

The handwriting is enormous and erratic, the pen sliding from broad to sharp and back, unpunctuated, running over the page in a way so uneven as to express his panic. After almost two years of suffering, on January 11, 1836, Eliza died. She was twenty-five, he thirty-one. Happiness had been ripped out of his life.

Her death was the second determining event in Robert's life. He wrote in the front of his Bible, "I am left to pursue the remainder of my pilgrimage alone – and in the waste that lies before me, I can expect to find joy only in the reflected happiness of our darling children, and in looking forward in humble hope, to that blessed hour which by God's permission shall forever reunite me to my Eliza in the world of spirits."

Robert made other notations in the front of his prayer book, including favourite prayers. The cover and the few outside pages are worn and broken, while the pages inside seem to have been scarcely opened. It is as if he were worshipping Eliza well before God.

There are two dried leaves slipped between the pages. A fern marks the table of Affinity, which lays out whom a man may and may not marry, as if his most secret agony is that he brought on Eliza's death by marrying his first cousin, as if their consummated love were a mortal sin in the full sense. The second leaf lies in the middle of the Psalms, as if the six on the two pages are a guide to his state of being, to his suffering – "mine eye is consumed with grief, yea, my soul and my belly" – as the basis for what will follow; "[m]y life is spent with grief, and my years with sighing." And to his sense of public purpose: "He hath shewed me his marvellous kindness in a strong city." And from that strong city of love he can triumph. "Let not them that are mine enemies wrongfully rejoice over me ... Let them shout for joy and be glad, that favour my righteous course." But Eliza is his true religion; God and his texts are mere support material.

The room in which she died in the Front Street house became the martyr's altar of his personal cult. He went in every day alone. No one saw it until, according to Cross and Fraser, thirteen years later, in 1849, when his daughter Maria turned twenty-one. He was then in effect deputy prime minister, in the midst of his greatest political crisis. The government of Canada had just been moved from riot-torn Montreal to Toronto. Maria, fully bilingual, was acting as his personal assistant, particularly on French–English matters and advising him in private.

The cult of Eliza involved two feast days: May 31, their wedding anniversary, and January 11, the day of her death. Around these dates he could rarely function as a public man. He would walk, as in a pilgrimage, from one site of their courtship and life together to the next; in January he would trudge these kilometres whatever the weather. And on any day that he was at Spadina, their country house, he could look out at the mausoleum in which she lay waiting for him. He never left the house without some of her love letters in his pocket, to read discreetly at any moment, in a meeting, sitting in Parliament, at the end of the day in bed. He feared that he might die suddenly without something of her close to his body.

Eliza's death hardened him to the reality of the world. Yes, his family remained. But now he was increasingly driven by what lay outside, by the needs of the public good, as if that were the intended consequence of her sacrifice and his despair. It could not be for nothing, this loss of their happiness. The certainty he brought to the public sphere had nothing to do with ideological blinders; nor was it a product, as among the Orangemen and later the Grits, of Protestant rigidity and self-righteousness, with its underpinning of predestination. An Anglican on the surface, he was if anything a spiritualist. And while these private affairs of belief and suffering made him the kind of man he was, he did not allow them to limit his idea of the public good. He separated in his mind and his policies not only church from state, but personal demons from state. This ability was rare for the time. He felt that he had no longer anything to lose. And so he would engage in politics for the cause, for the ideas he believed in – an immeasurable strength in a political world where self-interest and confused purpose dominated. When others would bend on basic principles, he would hold firm while manoeuvring on the surface. When they believed the best service to their cause was to cling to power, he was always ready to walk out the door. That clarity of spirit gave him the force to do what he felt was necessary.

WHILE ROBERT BALDWIN was living out his happiness and agony, the tension in Upper Canada steadily grew. Early in the century the Family Compact held sway. The Assembly, even when controlled by reformers, was treated as little more than a debating chamber. The Compact had the power. They could ignore the words. And the governors – all of them – from John Graves Simcoe on, backed the Compact. Or rather, the governors kept the Compact *loyal* by providing them with income through official positions and contracts, and so maintained real control. None of the governors were democrats, whatever their other qualities. None of them believed in local power. Nor did their masters in London. Power was something London lent to governors, who hid behind the symbol of the monarch as evidence of loyalty, in order to disperse the temporary use of it to local favourites for their financial self-interest.

But the second wave of reformers under William Warren Baldwin, Marshall Bidwell and John Rolph began to consolidate their popular position. The oligarchs in Toronto,

Kingston and a few other towns were outnumbered by the farmers, all of whom had the vote and used it.

In 1833 a young businessman called Francis Hincks rented a Baldwin house on Yonge Street and quickly became a family friend. He was bilingual, knew something about francophone reform leaders and was full of ideas. He wanted change, had few prejudices, was full of energy and had an optimistic view of what was possible.

The 1820s and 1830s were like a pressure cooker with the dial gradually turning up. The opposition gradually consolidated its forces. The Compact responded with anger. Relatively genteel elections became increasingly violent. In the early 1830s, William Lyon Mackenzie was repeatedly elected to the legislature and expelled. The reform movement rallied behind him. In 1834 they carried the first Toronto municipal election, and these new aldermen elected Mackenzie the first mayor. He created and chaired a commission to look into public finances, to the great embarrassment of the Compact. But he was a terrible administrator and so lasted only a year.

It was over these same decades that the idea of Responsible Government emerged. Locked in their Whig perception of politics and desperate not to frighten London, the reformers constantly presented this idea as the mere transferral of a British constitutional principle. Robert, with his talent for conceptual argument, gradually became its clarifier and salesman. Their strategy was to make Responsible Government appear to be self-evident and British; a government must have the confidence of the house in order to govern. Without confidence, it must fall. The government is not the creature of the governor any more than in London it was the creature of the King.

The reformers, including the Baldwins, did not at first understand the implications of their own argument. The development of full parliamentary democracy has two halves. First, the will of the people is expressed through their suffrage. Canada already had as full an expression of that as the nineteenth century could imagine. We had virtually universal male suffrage because most males were land-owning farmers and so met the property requirements of the day. Such extensive franchise did not exist in the United States given its half slave-based economy, existed only periodically in France, and even after the 1832 reform bill in London, suffrage had only been extended to a small part of the middle class for the simple reason that few men owned property.

The second half of parliamentary democracy's ascension was that the people's suffrage produced a legislature that could give or withdraw its confidence from the government.

The government would thus live or die. But such a clear principle had not yet been established in Britain or anywhere else. And so the clarity of the idea put forward by the Baldwins, combined with universal male suffrage, was frightening to many people.

The reformers said they were Whigs, but full parliamentary democracy was not a Whig idea – that is, it was not about power shifting between two competing elites. It was about power passing to the citizenry. The Tories were right. Such a transfer would effectively mark the end of British power in Canada and so the end of their own access to it. Why would the largest empire in the world and their local acolytes agree to that?

The final drama was still twelve years away, when, on January 23, 1836, a new Lieutenant-Governor arrived in Toronto. Sir Edmund Bond Head seemed so inappropriate, even ridiculous, in his egotism, conceits and manners as to have been chosen by mistake. Or perhaps his arrival was an expression of the colonial office's contempt for the colonial voter and the reformers. Eliza had been dead two weeks. The governor almost immediately asked Robert to join his Executive Council. It has often been argued that he was distracted by his mourning and so mishandled what followed. It could more easily be argued that Robert, with a new level of intellectual severity, took the governor through a process demonstrating that government from the top could not work. He was developing an instinctive sense of how to move his principles forward.

After a quick negotiation Robert agreed to join the three Compact representatives on the Council, provided that he could bring two reformers on with him. They were sworn in on February 20. There was one reform condition, verbally agreed to by the governor: that Responsible Government be applied. Bond Head then refused to send the written confirmation of this agreement. Robert therefore quickly convinced all five of the other councillors that they had been treated with contempt, made fools of. The entire Council resigned in protest. The Assembly backed them by withholding supplies – money – to the government. And so the final spiral into disorder began.

The criticism of Robert was that he had been too brittle, hadn't held on to power, was too prickly for the real world. In other words, he had not acted like a Whig. True. Instead, he had demonstrated that false compromise did not serve the public good.

Bond Head called an election. William Warren and Francis Hincks organized the Constitutional Reform Society to fight back. William Lyon Mackenzie had already given up on the process and was writing to Louis-Joseph Papineau and Denis-Benjamin Viger, the reform leaders in Montreal, to create an alliance that would eventually lead to two badly organized and badly coordinated rebellions. And Egerton Ryerson, the Methodist leader and advocate of public education, made one of the two biggest mistakes of his career. During the election he backed the governor and the Compact in the expectation that this support would somehow advance his causes. The reformers were defeated, and the most frustrated among them moved toward rebellion.

Robert had simply walked away from all of this. Within a month of his resignation he had sailed for England, leaving his children in the care of his mother. In London the colonial secretary, Lord Glenelg, refused to see him. He was fobbed off on Lord John Russell. Nevertheless, Robert wrote what would become a historic letter to Glenelg, setting out both the situation and the solution, carefully choosing language that London might be able to digest. Yet his language was cool, even cold, without any provincial forelock-tugging: "If it is the desire of the Mother Country to retain the colony … it can only be done either by force or with the consent of the people. I take it for granted that Great Britain cannot desire to exercise a Government of the Sword."

He went on to lay out the remedy – Responsible

Government – and ended by warning of disorder to come. He appealed to British self-respect and intelligence. "Your Luddship must adapt the government to the genius of the people upon and among whom it is to act."

He then left for Ireland and Cork to examine his family's past, but above all to think about his life after Eliza's death. What effect did this ten-month trip have? He concluded that he liked Ireland but had no desire to spend more time there. He didn't particularly like England and noted that even the more informed of the English knew nothing of Canada and cared even less – "Most of [them] seemed rarely to have had the fact of the existence of such a country present to their minds."

He meditated upon Eliza, tried to imagine how he would bring up his children – in reality Phoebe, his own mother, would run their lives. And she believed in a strong intellectual education for girls. She had herself painted with Maria, the eldest daughter, both of them reading books. The message was calculated. This was one of the first Canadian paintings of women reading. Meanwhile in Ireland, Robert was thinking about family. To William Warren he wrote, "I know I am loved as father – brother – nephew – cousin – friend.... Oh, my father, this family love is a holy and blessed affection; let us cherish it." The weight of his melancholy came through in his letters and in a rare and worried letter that his mother wrote – "My Dear Dear child" – in a long attempt to reassure him. In all of this correspondence you can feel his confusion – confusion on all fronts, particularly politics. He is a reformer but cannot bring himself to engage fully. Why? Perhaps because the cause does not make sense as it stands.

Early in 1837 he is back in Toronto, "my own, my native land." The political pressure cooker is about to explode, yet he withdraws yet again, yet again to concentrate on family and, above all, on his cult of Eliza. Over the summer Mackenzie and Papineau are regularly citing each other's words at public meetings, admiring each other's movements, egging each other on, as if to demonstrate that they are not alone.

In late November, rebellion breaks out in Lower Canada. One battle is won against the British at Saint-Denis under the Patriote leadership of Wolfred Nelson and George-Étienne Cartier, friends of LaFontaine, as they will later be of Baldwin. Mackenzie then launches his own rebellion. Eight hundred farmers, some armed, advance on Toronto down Yonge Street. Robert agrees to ride north out through the forest with John Rolph to see if negotiations are possible. He does not know that Rolph is secretly the rebellion leader. There is a strained meeting with Mackenzie and

Samuel Lount about two kilometres north of Bloor Street. Mackenzie insists that any offer of a truce must be in writing. Robert and Rolph ride back to the governor's mansion. Bond Head withdraws the offer. They ride back out, and there is an even more confused conversation, with Rolph quietly encouraging Mackenzie to attack the city.

It must have been there, isolated on the country road riding back and forth between two armed camps of fellow citizens, that Robert began to experience his third seismic event. Later that day there would be a disastrous skirmish with a few men killed. Both sides were acting out a script written on another continent. Neither side was a reflection of what was possible here. And when he saw the eight hundred farmers, idealistic, ready to risk their lives, what impact did it have? Within hours he would discover that Rolph, his old law partner and fellow neutral messenger, was actually the rebel leader. In the city he was faced by the arbitrary egotism of the governor, shaping the lives of people for whom he cared nothing. Over the days and weeks that followed he had to watch the arrest of over a thousand fellow citizens, many of them people he knew. Others fled to the United States, including Mackenzie, Bidwell and Rolph, all of his former political allies.

What did this say about the philosophical road he and his

father and the other reformers had been going down for years? If it had led to this catastrophe, it could not be the right road. They could not simply blame an idiotic governor and the Compact or even the foolishness of Mackenzie. There was something wrong about the way they had imagined the future of Upper Canada.

Robert spent the spring as the lead defence lawyer for the rebels, trial after trial. John Beverley Robinson, the senior figure of the Compact and the chief justice, presided over the trials. Robert fought for the lives of these men, one by one. Two were hanged. For many others he managed to win acquittal. Ninety-three were sent to Van Diemen's Land, now Tasmania, the cruellest place in Australia, where most disappeared forever into virtual slavery.

What did Robert Baldwin draw from all of this? That he was not a Whig. That Whigs, like Tories, saw politics as a shapeless mechanism of power. Each vaunted a particular form of common sense. But these were mere negotiating positions to do with contracts and authority, particularly when it came to dealing with colonies. This was a method designed by a people jammed together on their island. These imported theories could not work here. What could? A broad strategy proper to this place. He did not yet know what it was.

CHAPTER THREE

Out from Under the Master's Shadow

It is widely thought that the personality of a boy whose father dies is deeply affected. He often becomes intensely driven, unusually combative or aggressive, as if making up for the conversation never to be had or the rivalry never to be played out, as if searching for a replacement father or attempting to become himself the omniscient head of family. Pierre Trudeau comes to mind, or René Lévesque.

Louis-Hippolyte LaFontaine was born October 4, 1807, in Boucherville, a rich seigneurie on the south shore of the St. Lawrence, downriver from Montreal. Robert Baldwin was three years old. In Boucherville, the Europeans had once again grafted themselves on to a First Nations settlement on the shore of the river behind the protection of an archipelago of islands. Six years later Louis-Hippolyte's father abruptly died. Within months his mother remarried.

Louis-H, as he was commonly called by his friends, had been born in a squared-timber house in one of those narrow strip farms running down to the river. His stepfather's house, immediately next door, was built of stone. We know nothing about these relationships except that his mother, by remarrying, had moved quickly to protect her children. Later the stone house would be left to Louis-H's sister and her farming husband. This development was hardly surprising. Why leave the property to a rising legal star in Montreal? On the other hand, there are no real signs of any sort of close relationship with his family as he grew older. It would be easy to misread this as the story of an ambitious young man leaving his habitant family behind. In reality, both his grandfather and his father had been captains of the local militia. His grandfather had also been an MP. They were habitants – peasant farmers – on a seigneurie, but they were also community leaders.

Perhaps they didn't get on. Louis-Hippolyte was certainly a tempestuous young man. Perhaps the stepfather had the simple misfortune of not being the father. Whatever the reason, Louis-Hippolyte carried neither the advantages nor the disadvantages of family life with him into adulthood.

With neither a father nor a functioning blood-and-flesh family, he spent much of his life seeking a replacement, a situation evident in his relationship with the nationalist leader Louis-Joseph Papineau and in his immediate affection for William Warren Baldwin.

He was a brilliant student and so was plucked out, aged thirteen, to board at the Collège de Montréal, a large H-shaped stone building, three storeys high, on Rue Saint-Paul just west of McGill Street, on the edge of the city core. A hundred-metre walk would bring the boys down to the port, probably the liveliest place in town. If they were to walk a hundred metres straight into town they would come to the building site of the Marché Sainte-Anne, designed as the grandest building in Montreal. It would be converted into the Canadian Parliament in the mid-1840s. Another hundred metres would bring them to the Pointe-à-Callière, site of the First Nations settlement on the banks of the St. Lawrence where Montreal was first established.

The Collège de Montréal was one of two breeding grounds for francophone leaders, the other being the Seminary in Quebec City. The Collège offered a classical elite education far more sophisticated than anything available to anglophones anywhere in Canada. Louis-Hippolyte was there for five years, leaving in 1824 to become a law clerk. Almost immediately, aged eighteen, he threw himself into political activism by writing for *La Minèrve*, run by another ex-student, Augustin-Norbert Morin. Twenty-five years later, in the autumn of 1851, Morin, the incoming Canadian prime minister, would chair a banquet in

Montreal to honour LaFontaine, the outgoing prime minister. LaFontaine reminded the aging banqueters that in the 1820s men went into politics very young. There was an urgent need for commitment.

And he had been a driven young man – argumentative, opinionated, constantly working, with a remarkable memory. He loved sports, particularly "real tennis" – jeu de pelote – which is dependent on speed, agility and a sustained toughness, as the ball is hit with the player's hand. His nickname at the Collège de Montréal had been La Grosse Tête, a double reference to brains and to his impressive large head, with a broad forehead, reminiscent of those stylized statues of Roman emperors. The name stuck because of the role he played among his contemporaries.

As a law clerk he lived with François Roy, a well-known lawyer under whom he was training. They passed their time talking politics, arguing, playing against each other in jeu de pelote. LaFontaine had discovered his first stand-in father. Four years later he was called to the bar. He was twenty-one.

In 1830 he could be found marching through the streets with other young men, a French tricolour ribbon in their buttonholes to celebrate the revolution in Paris that had brought down the Bourbon monarchy. Like all French revolutions it ended in a counter-revolution. Those in Montreal who set their mental clock by European ideas and events would see this result as just another temporary setback. For LaFontaine we can only suspect this was a first signal that the solution to Canadian problems might not be importable.

A few months later he was elected to the legislature of Lower Canada for the riding of Terrebonne, north of Montreal. He arrived just as the tensions between the Reform Party and the Château Clique – the equivalent of the Family Compact – were rising to unsustainable levels. It was precisely the same struggle as in Upper Canada, with the added complexity of language and a different religious balance.

In Upper Canada the struggle between the reformers and the Family Compact often felt like an incipient civil war, with enemies sitting across from each other in the same churches and belonging to the same associations. In Lower Canada, in spite of the often successful francophone-anglophone power sharing of the 1791 constitution, the anglophone elite increasingly attempted to use what they defined as a difference of race to justify their minority controlling political and therefore economic power. Of course it wasn't really about race. From the Château Clique's point of view it was about power and money. But their interests were presented as Protestant versus Catholic and English-speaker versus French-speaker. These were the traditional European divisions imported into the colony and presented as symbols of loyalty versus disloyalty. As with the Family Compact in Upper Canada, so with the Château Clique in Lower Canada: their mechanism for the maintenance of power was the governor. From this they concluded that loyalty to the Crown was by definition anti-democratic. In Lower Canada they had the added argument that as anglophones they were by definition loyal, and a non–Anglo Saxon, reformer or not, could not be.

Within the same year as his election, 1830, LaFontaine was married to Adèle Berthelot, the daughter of a rich businessman. At twenty-three he was an increasingly successful lawyer, a member of Parliament and part of a financially powerful family. It was an interesting marriage. Adèle's father had never married. She was adopted, as was her brother. There are strong hints that both were his children out of wedlock. The mother was never mentioned. It is as if LaFontaine and Adèle were drawn to each other in part by their messy, unsatisfactory family backgrounds. Their marriage had a modern feel about it. She acted as his equal, not the classic nineteenth-century supportive wife. She played an interesting role in the political campaigns of the 1830s. While he was in exile after the failed uprising, she was very publicly – courageously – at the centre of the work to support the prisoners. During their twenty-eight years together they were devoted to each other.

RELIGION AND LANGUAGE ASIDE, the European settlements of Lower Canada were much older than those in Upper Canada and so the political divisions were more structured and solidified. The change of imperial regime from French to English had given political weapons to both sides. The local English – who were mainly Scots and Irish and not English at all – would claim racial loyalty to the monarch. But the reform movement, led by but not at all exclusive to the French Canadians, would claim their right to English constitutional rights – a concept that was not even a theoretical possibility in the colonies of other empires. For that matter, the legitimate claims that francophone Catholics were making would not have been possible in Britain itself or elsewhere in Europe. The British/European nation-states were increasingly being built on the domination of one race, language, religion over all others. They had already been killing each other for two centuries in order to create their individual fictions of the monolithic nation-state. They would go on killing each other for the same reasons until 1945. The singular oddity of the Canadian colonies was that

the Quebec Act of 1773 and the 1791 constitution guaranteed Catholics and francophones every colonial right that
any anglophone Protestant might claim, just as the Royal
Proclamation of 1763 guaranteed First Nations' rights.

The cry of the reformers had for decades been cool and
precise – *respect the constitution* – while the Château Clique,
like the Family Compact in Toronto, could only hide their
crude desire for power and money behind the vague, romantic theory of racial loyalty. But again, all empires were organized around romantic racial loyalty, whether British, French,
German or American. There was always some noble dis-
course about British constitutional principles or Liberté,
Egalité, Fraternité, or the civilization of the Holy Roman
Empire, or Life, Liberty and the Pursuit of Happiness. But
when it came to their colonies it was all about race and
power.

There was one other fairly classic factor. The Montreal
Anglo merchant class was for the most part deeply uninter-
esting and ill-educated. These merchants made the same
mistake vis-à-vis French Canada that the Protestant Boston
merchants had made in the 1760s. They thought that
because their kind and their side had won the war, they
were, therefore, in the manner of crude medieval barons,
owed the spoils of war. They simply weren't capable of

understanding that the game being played, given the sophistication of the reform elite, might really be about the will of the people and the rule of law.

The situation into which LaFontaine slipped as an MP was almost deliciously contradictory. Lower Canada, like Upper Canada, was deeply egalitarian. But class, nevertheless, did exist. And the leader of the reform movement, Louis-Joseph Papineau, was an aristocrat by wealth, social position, education, mannerisms, by the cut and quality of his clothes. That didn't mean he was cut off in the European manner from the rest of the population. His father had made a fortune, but his father's father had been a farmer, and this was, as I said, an egalitarian society. In some ways Louis-Joseph resembled William Warren Baldwin. They were both intelligent Enlightenment-style Whigs. In some ways Louis-Joseph was a combination of William Warren and William Lyon Mackenzie, particularly as he and Mackenzie were great public tribunes, not just great parliamentary speakers. Their power lay in their abilities outdoors before crowds of thousands. The irony was that Papineau found himself in a political struggle that was shaped in part by the British class system, with power and authority devolving as if naturally from a monarch through an aristocratic political class in Britain to a governor in each colony, who himself was treated like a monarch. His colonial advisers – the Château Clique and the Family Compact – were the natural beneficiaries of this pyramidal system. But Papineau was the political leader in early-nineteenth-century Lower Canada who had the royal jelly. He actually was the aristocrat that the Clique and Compact members were pretending to be.

LaFontaine was at Papineau's side during public events in part because the young man was strong and aggressive. In 1832 there was a by-election in Montreal involving the worst riots anyone had seen. A number of French Canadians were killed. LaFontaine was the one chosen to stay close to the leader when he found himself in the middle of the pandemonium. But he was also thought to be particularly smart and thought of himself that way. Physically and intellectually he demonstrated self-confidence. Add to that the brashness of a very young man and you can understand that some of Papineau's older disciples resented him. He joined the little group of intellectual reform leaders, including Papineau and George-Étienne Cartier, who met regularly to discuss strategy at Édouard Fabre's bookstore on the corner of Notre-Dame and Rue Saint-Vincent, a block west of Place Jacques-Cartier.

LaFontaine was soon travelling with Papineau to public meetings in smaller towns. He was writing letters and documents for his leader. Papineau had truly become his father figure.

In 1834 the Lower Canadian Assembly passed the 92 Resolutions, a list of grievances and demands to be sent to the British government. This was the first charter of the democratic movement. It was not a republican argument or a declaration of independence. The 92 Resolutions used the Whig idea of loyalty to British constitutional principles as a norm from which to insist on justice. They were rejected by London, thus setting in motion the process that would lead to rebellion in 1837.

In 1834 two leading reformers, the brothers Mondelet, betrayed the reform cause by accepting office from the governor and opposing the 92 Resolutions. LaFontaine published a violent attack on them, "Les deux girouettes ou l'hypocrisie démasquée" (Two weather vanes or hypocrisy unmasked), seventy-five pages of closely argued hyperbole. It was considered to be an important political event. He followed this with a long pamphlet attacking the power of priests in Lower Canada.

By 1837 no constitutional progress had been made and so the reformers used their majority in the House to refuse the civil list – that is, they refused to pay the salaries of the civil service. In March the British government responded to this refusal with their own 10 Resolutions, which simply negated the role of the colonial Assembly. Interestingly enough, Lord John Russell, the father of the 1832 English Reform Bill, was personally responsible for this refusal of democratic reform in London's leading colony. Democracy for Britain did not mean democracy for Canada. This distinction was part of a long-established pattern.

The reformers retaliated with a campaign to boycott goods. Papineau and LaFontaine appeared in public wearing clothing made of locally woven cloth, as did Adèle LaFontaine. When a journalist made fun of her, LaFontaine sought him out and in public knocked him to the ground with a solid punch. Papineau and LaFontaine in country clothing led the way into Parliament for its opening in August. After eight days of argument, Gosford, the Governor General, dissolved Parliament. Papineau's house, just around the corner from the Château Ramezay, was under threat from an organization of young Tories, and LaFontaine was one of the young men defending it. In October Wolfred Nelson chaired a great public reform meeting of five thousand people. Within the month fighting was under way. On November 24 Nelson and Cartier led the local citizens to victory over British troops in the Battle of Saint-Denis. The next day the British won in an uneven contest over the Patriotes, led by Thomas Storrow Brown, at Saint-Charles. A week later the local forces of the most powerful army in the world had got their act together, and the rebellion was over. Papineau had already fled to the United States. As in Upper Canada, it had all happened in an atmosphere of total confusion.

Papineau would later insist that he had never wanted the protests to come to violence. And in fairness he was a tribune, not a military or a political leader. The word has great power as long as the guns are not fired. He had carried most of Lower Canada with the nobility of his language of justice, and his followers loyally followed. But the British ceded nothing on any point. And so the rhetoric, by its own force and its effect on the people, began to race toward violence. Papineau had failed to understand this dynamic and failed to do anything about it. He fled the scene of the Battle of Saint-Denis in confused circumstances, an action that would damage his reputation. One thing is clear: neither Mackenzie nor Papineau ever came to terms with their personal failure as leaders and therefore their personal responsibility for the catastrophes.

LaFontaine remained loyal to Papineau through it all, even though he early on began to doubt the strategy. In public he was as aggressive as everyone else. In private, however,

LaFontaine was insisting on the impossibility of success through arms. As early as February 17, 1837, he was writing in letters that violence could not work against an empire. He proposed passive resistance – "[une] force d'inertie." "That I believe is the line that Lower Canada will be forced to take." The British product boycott, support of local products and the idea of passive resistance – these were the elements used by Gandhi a century later.

LaFontaine's letters show that he sensed they were on a road to failure. They had to find another strategy, one that drew back from the vortex of fighting the most powerful empire in the world on an open plain. He suggested that the abolition of seigneurial rights would be a way of uniting the people around a cause that would strengthen their self-esteem and their place in modern society. And it would be a way of weakening the Château Clique, since many of the seigneuries had been bought up by the Scottish merchants. "The government, the seigneurs and the jumped-up pretend aristocrats in both parties will probably oppose it, but the masses will unite around the cause and act as one; and perhaps by understanding better that their interests are one, they will no longer be divided in politics.... I defy the government to try to hold back such a popular will." Papineau would have been horrified. Even fifteen years later, in his last manifestation as leader of the young radicals, he was still defending his rights as a seigneur.

As 1837 unravelled, LaFontaine began to discover the other side of his own character. Yes, he was combative, argumentative, physical, but he also had a hard, cool idea of strategy. He didn't mind a tough situation. But he didn't like to lose. The essence of good strategy is not to put yourself in a hopeless situation. His friends were caught up in the drama: Papineau and his advisers, mesmerized by their own rhetoric; the brothers Wolfred and John Nelson, angry and preparing for battle, supported by young men like George-Étienne Cartier, more restrained figures like Étienne Parent drawing back in despair.

LaFontaine's aggressive self-confidence and sense of strategy led him to attempt to fill the void uninvited, almost alone. His problem was that he did not yet have a strategy for the long term. And it would have to be a very new approach. He was as deeply confused as everyone else. What he did have was enough willpower and sense of risk to try some defensive tactics in an attempt to minimize the impending catastrophe.

And so a few days before the fighting he wrote urgently to the governor, imploring him to recall Parliament: a return to the words of debate was the only way to prevent fighting.

"La paix avant tout." "The only effective way to return peace in this country is to recall Parliament. One hundred times better to rule thanks to the confidence and love of the people than through force." He admitted to his closest friend, law partner and his wife's cousin, Joseph-Amable Berthelot, that he had little hope. "We are convinced that they will not do it; but [we must show London] that we wish at least to keep the legislature. Our opponents are moving heaven and earth to ensure we no longer have an assembly."

He was entirely right about the Assembly. The Château Clique's dream was to remove all democratic rights from francophones. LaFontaine admitted that his intervention was a desperate last gamble. He wrote to the governor on November 19. On December 23, as the noose of martial law tightened, he and Augustin-Norbert Morin slipped out of Quebec City, crossing the river by canoe through the ice floes, then headed south by sleigh under heavy furs, sliding through forests in the middle of the night. LaFontaine and Morin separated near the border, Morin heading back home, where he would keep his head down. LaFontaine crossed into the United States on Christmas Day and sailed from New York for London a week later, hoping to plead the case for justice and the recall of the Assembly in Lower Canada. The last news he received as he went on board was of more friends being arrested.

Again, this was a self-imposed mission, but he arrived in London just as the House of Commons had voted to suspend the Canadian constitution. For a month he lobbied as best he could, never quite sure whether a warrant existed for his arrest. When one was finally issued he slipped off to Paris, where he would spend three months, peppering British officials with letters, fretting in his diary, always about the situation at home. He didn't want to be an exile.

Throughout the wet, grey winter he walked endlessly, almost maniacally, about Paris, meeting anyone who might be useful, going to the theatre to distract himself. He had strong views for and against the plays he saw and the acting style then in fashion. There was one strange new factor. He was sick almost all the time. It gradually emerged that he was suffering from inflammatory rheumatism, which causes joints to swell and such pain that sufferers cannot move for weeks. Boils follow in the swollen joints, along with severe chest pains and very high fevers. It is a disease that kills through infections and blood clots. LaFontaine was only thirty-one, compulsively active. Now he found himself confined to bed for days, often weeks.

From the moment he had sat down in the canoe to cross between the ice floes of the St. Lawrence, it was as if he were entering into a period of introspection interrupted only by the need for immediate tactical action. Unlike Papineau, who stayed away until 1845, a year after LaFontaine managed to get him a pardon, the younger man wished only to get home. In his diary during the long crossing of the Atlantic away from Canada he had reflected on belonging. "Someone who says he is a citizen of the world is lying about the inspiration of his soul." But he had no new strategy and was reduced to focusing on essential details, continually calling for the release of the prisoners and a general amnesty. Writing from Paris to a supporter in London about the British class system and Canada, he noted, "You will not succeed in establishing an aristocracy where it does not know how to exist." He referred to the opposition of such elites to universal suffrage as "le moribund aux prise avec la mort" – the half-dead struggling with death.

When he learned that a new Governor General, Lord Durham, famous liberal and author of the 1832 British Reform Bill, had sailed for Canada in the spring of 1838, he himself followed immediately. This same optimism overwhelmed reformers throughout Lower and Upper Canada. In a last letter from Paris to London LaFontaine continued his lobbying: "The right policy to follow toward Canada is one of progress. Otherwise, rule by military force. But then your rule will last no longer than any government held up by bayonets."

Adèle was waiting for him in New York. She had been a regular presence in Montreal's prison, filled as it was with their friends. She had been the prisoners' main source of food, writing materials, even artists' equipment, and perhaps more important she was their contact with the world outside.

LaFontaine immediately wrote to Dominick Daly, a member of the governor's Executive Council, warning him that he was coming home, calling for a general amnesty and setting out the basis for the future struggle. They could exercise the warrant against him if they wished, but they had to allow him to defend his case in public before a proper court. He was not afraid of a trial; he wanted one; he looked forward to it with pleasure. And he sent copies of his letter to MPs in England. The message is clear: *go on, arrest me; you'll have to deal with the consequences.* On his way north to the border he spent an evening in Saratoga with Papineau and his friends, including George-Étienne Cartier. With the exception of Cartier they were clearly annoyed by the enthusiasm with which he was heading back into the fray. They all had warrants against them, but LaFontaine was ready to risk crossing the border. And Cartier would soon follow. A letter written about this evening by one of Papineau's friends has a clear tone: who does he think he is? As for LaFontaine, he now knew what he thought of the older leaders. He wrote privately to a friend: "I blame them for what they did." He had heard that they were against the violence, but "Papineau could have prevented it. Not to have done so, he should have stayed to fight. The habitants are calling for [Wolfred] Nelson. They embrace those who have not abandoned them in combat."

LaFontaine said nothing of this in public. The shadow of Papineau as a stand-in father remained. And LaFontaine believed deeply in personal loyalty and in solidarity among those who fought for justice. LaFontaine's disagreements and filial disappointment on one side, and on the other Papineau's annoyance at having failed and been replaced, would remain draped in silence for another decade.

ON JUNE 23, 1838, LaFontaine and Adèle arrived in Montreal, and he threw himself into defending the prisoners and leading a campaign for general amnesty. He bombarded the governor, the jailors, British politicians with letters. It is difficult to imagine now, but from 1838 to 1841 Lower Canada existed outside what could be called law. A small anglophone minority held power and used it to imprison and impoverish their enemies. It was one of those rare completely

European moments in Canadian history when one group thought they could get away with reformulating the country as if no one else existed.

LaFontaine had no sooner arrived than eight of his allies, then in jail, were banished by Lord Durham to Bermuda. This number included Wolfred Nelson. At the time it seemed as if they would be gone forever. Nelson wrote constantly to LaFontaine, in part to thank him for his support, in part to thank Adèle – "votre excellente dame" – for all her prison work and to thank the LaFontaines several times for offering to adopt one of his children – "my dear orphans." The child in question was probably his youngest boy, who would grow up to be a doctor. Nelson's wife was faced with poverty, as his property had been seized and she had seven children to raise. The adoption didn't happen, but the two families grew increasingly close. By now the LaFontaines realized they would not have children and shifted their family focus to supporting children in difficulty.

In effect, by throwing himself into the centre of people's suffering and by taking on their defence, LaFontaine had become the new leader. He had become the voice of the Patriotes.

On November 2 Robert Nelson led a force across the

LOUIS-HIPPOLYTE LaFONTAINE AND ROBERT BALDWIN

border from New York in the hope of provoking a second
rebellion. It was a disastrously organized business. Soon
850 had been arrested. On Sunday morning, the fourth,
LaFontaine came out of Notre Dame after Mass with Adèle
and many friends. Soldiers were waiting to arrest the men.
It is hard for us now to feel what it must have felt like for
them. There they were, respectable community leaders –
lawyers, doctors, teachers, businessmen – dressed for Mass
in the great basilica that still stands on Place d'Armes. They
were with their wives, mothers, children. Of course they
knew there was new trouble, but that was hundreds of kilometres away. They strolled out, perhaps on their way to a
family lunch, exchanging what they had heard about the
disaster. And there were the armed soldiers, who began
rounding them up. What would the wives, the children
have felt, seeing the men picked up in this way? LaFontaine
in one of his letters of protest said they had been seized like
stray dogs.

It was as if he had been waiting for this moment.
LaFontaine had continually dared the authorities to arrest
him. Now, by improperly depriving him of his citizen rights,
those in control handed him an ideal platform for fighting
back on behalf of the much larger cause. He applied the
principles of British law to fight a rogue power that claimed

British authority. The arrests were so incompetently done from a legal standpoint that he was able to mock his opponents from behind bars. They hadn't used a warrant. The ordinance they cited didn't yet exist. There were no specific accusations.

To Lord Brougham, a British MP, he sent a message on December 3, 1838: "Today I write you from the depths of prison.… All the cruelty and injustices that you commit are only to prop up a little urban oligarchy."

To Sir John Colborne, administrateur du gouvernement du Bas-Canada, December 3, 1837: "I can only imagine that there is some sort of accusation against me, perhaps put together after the fact. Whatever. The accusation of high treason seems to be in fashion. No doubt that will be it. Well! I solemnly demand from Your Excellency my trial before a tribunal which is legal and constitutional in my country. I demand it as a right, as I believe that these rights do still exist in the written law."

To Sir John Colborne, December 18, 1838: "A people only revolt when it can no longer support the intolerable weight of oppression and tyranny. Unfortunate victims are in irons. A court martial has condemned them to death. Sir, this death will be a political death. What will be the result? Peace? I doubt it. Do you want peace? Well then, spill no blood on the scaffold. Blood is the inexhaustible seed of revolution."

And on and on. He turned himself and his fellow prisoners into a political force – an embarrassment to the British.

Eventually most were released, but in February of 1839, twelve were hanged. Fifty-eight were sent to Australia. And then the Durham Report was released.

LaFontaine had waited for this outcome with optimism. Surely such a voice of liberalism and democracy would understand the intolerable situation in which they lived. And indeed the new governor did offer both liberalism and democracy – however, only if the francophones evaporated. They were simply to disappear as a political reality. French was to vanish as a legal public language, and francophones were to lose their real majority in the population, as the two Canadas were to be put together with equal seats for each.

In other words, Durham's democratic formula was a version of the Family Compact's anti-democratic formula. There would be democracy, but for the anglophones only. What LaFontaine had missed in all of his courageous politics was that there was no such thing as an international application for British democratic principles. That is the nature of any empire. It was true of the French in Haiti or

Algeria, the United States in the Philippines, Germany, and Italy in Africa. LaFontaine now found himself in a confusing vacuum. His tactics had helped many people. But these were tactics. He was the leader of his people and he had no convincing strategy.

CHAPTER FOUR

Finding Another Way

And so there they were, two youngish men, each in his own way the acknowledged leader of the embattled reform movement in his own colony. They had never met. They had never been to each other's city. And they were now, against their will, to belong to the same constitutional community.

They had heard a great deal about each other via newspapers, letters and reports from travellers. They knew, as did the reformers in the Maritimes, that their destinies were linked for at least one good reason: London, quite properly, would not develop a long-term colonial policy one colony at a time.

LaFontaine and Baldwin had survived an astonishing first decade of adulthood. As teenagers they had thrown themselves or been thrown into public life. Almost immediately they had been singled out as future leaders. The first half of the 1830s had been filled with hope – the creation of happy personal lives, the revelation of love, the expectation that the public situation could change for the better, the ease with which their legal and business careers had taken off.

The second half of the decade had brought a frightening decline – Baldwin was alone, without the one person he needed; LaFontaine and his wife were increasingly obsessed by their lack of children, the children they needed in order to create the kind of family neither had had. Political violence raged around both men, friends were hanged, shot, exiled, in and out of prison. The oligarchs were triumphant and using the failure of the radicals to squeeze the moderates. In the short term, the best that LaFontaine and Baldwin could do was devote their legal talents to saving as many of the victims as they could.

Everyone tends to simplify chaotic eras once they are over in order to extract a clear story of their evolution toward a predetermined destiny, good or bad. In truth, from mid-1837 to mid-1840, everything in Canada was chaos. The situation was worse in Lower Canada, where out-of-control mid-level British officers and local British volunteers burnt French-Canadian villages. The Château Clique got away with acting as a rogue government, arresting people at random, frightening people and bankrupting them by locking them up.

The standard story of Upper Canada is that the rebellion was brief and comic, with only two hangings, as opposed to a dozen in Lower Canada. In reality there were a series of uprisings, invasions and isolated troubles running through 1838. For example, at the time of Robert Nelson's invasion of Lower Canada in November, there was an invasion near Kingston leading to the drawn-out Battle of the Windmill. One hundred and twenty-six were killed, eleven executed, and another sixty transported to Australia.

In classic imperial terms, the francophones were an easy target. But in many ways it is more worrying for a racially based empire – and they usually are – when there is betrayal and rebellion from within the ruling race. Perhaps this explains why almost twice as many Upper Canadians were transported to Australia to truly destructive conditions in Van Diemen's Land, while the francophones got more standard treatment in Sydney and most survived to return home. Wolfred Nelson's group of eight sent to Bermuda were even treated with surprising dignity. On the other hand, the non-British reality of Lower Canada explains the more severe and prolonged removal of basic rights. Not being British, francophones had no racial entitlement to these rights.

So confusion still reigned in both Canadas when Durham arrived. Within days of his arrival he had amnestied most of the rebels and sent someone to talk to LaFontaine about expressing approval of the Governor General's actions. This approach LaFontaine carefully repulsed and set about defending the remaining prisoners. Within a month Durham was in Toronto and sitting down with the Baldwins, father and son, to get their advice. They were the *quality* of people whose advice might be receivable. All the same, it is hard to imagine the conversation. William Warren was then sixty-four, feeling old and impatient. Yes, he was a Whig patrician, but he was also deeply egalitarian in the Canadian way, and Responsible Government had been more or less his idea.

From their house on Front at Bay to the governor's residence in its formal gardens off King Street was a ten-minute carriage ride. They were given twenty minutes. Durham was intelligent, but flighty, unstable, overly certain of his destiny, overdressed. He would have found his two guests hard to read. Although members of the elite, they clearly had no time for the majority of their fellow Anglicans who led the Compact. And the son had been right in 1836 when in London he had written to the colonial secretary warning of a collapse into violence. In fact, the violence might have been avoided had the colonial secretary deigned to receive him.

Within days of the meeting both Baldwins had written Durham at length. Robert presented the argument for

Responsible Government in a way that a man of Durham's prejudices could digest. "Would the people of England endure any system of executive government over which they had less influence than that which at present exists? Your Lordship knows they would not." So why should we, loyal subjects, settle for less? Unless you wish us to become disloyal. "Your Lordship must adapt the government to the genius of the people upon and among whom it is to act."

Durham did integrate part of Baldwin's approach to Responsible Government into his report. But he didn't bother to sit down with any francophones. They weren't English. Which is not to say that he had any sympathy for the Family Compact or the Château Clique. They were vulgar colonials on the make. His report reflects all of these prejudices and emotions. Whatever he thought of the colonial nouveaux riches, he was careful to leave room for their continued financial success. The British Empire was built on commerce. The Compacts and Cliques – let's call them the compacts – were seen as a necessary evil. Yet here he missed the essential point. The compacts tended to attract the less original sort of businessmen who lived off government contracts. There was much more originality and drive and talent and taste for commercial risk on the reform side, francophone and anglophone.

For a few months in the middle of 1838 Durham managed to sustain a sense of hope about the possibility of future democracy. The prisons were emptying. Life was slowly moving toward some stability. Then he was gone, having resigned in a fit of pique over one difference with London. His ship left on November 1.

The next day came the incompetent invasions of both Upper and Lower Canada. Two days later came the spectacular arrests of LaFontaine and his friends on their way out of Notre Dame. He wasn't released until December 13, but Étienne Parent – the leading intellectual voice of the anti-violence moderates – was arrested two weeks later. There were executions in both colonies. And in the midst of these periodic hangings, the Durham Report was released. It was February 1839.

Joseph Howe, the leading journalist in Nova Scotia, read it and was converted to Responsible Government. He took up the cause, constantly writing about it in his newspaper, *The Novascotian*.

What Howe did mattered because he was famous throughout Lower and Upper Canada. In 1835 the Halifax Family Compact had tried to destroy both him and his newspaper. He had been criticizing their financial manipulations and profiteering, and many of them were judges.

They trumped up a charge of seditious libel that would have bankrupted him.

As I said earlier, countries develop patterns that reappear over time. In the late twentieth century, a small group of powerful men tried to shut down criticisms of themselves by launching repeated libel suits against writers and newspapers. It was a return of the old Compact approach and we called it libel chill.

Howe's trial took place in what is now the library of the Nova Scotia Legislature, a long, low room upstairs, jammed on this occasion, and very hot. He defended himself in a remarkable speech lasting almost five hours, exposing the financial details of the Compact's corruption, but much more important, laying out the philosophical and legal arguments for public justice, honesty and a responsible elite. Howe captured exactly the question of loyalty versus treason, which would be picked up by LaFontaine and then become central to the crisis of 1848–49. "When we hear the cry of disloyalty and disaffection raised in this colony … we cannot but smile at the cunning of those who, as they fail to satisfy the reason, seek to operate upon our fears.… He who robs the subject makes war upon the King; he who delays or withholds justice excites discontent and sedition; [the King] would tell them that they were the rebels." And he ended with a great peroration on the role of the citizen. "The only questions I ask myself are, What is right? What is just? What is for the public good?"

Howe was acquitted and thus laid the foundations for the Canadian idea of free speech. His concepts are reflected in today's Charter of Rights and Freedoms. Throughout the colonies his victory became a central mythological event in the rise of Canadian democracy. Why? His was the first major victory of the reformers over the compacts in any of the northern colonies – in fact, throughout the British Empire.

JUST AS JOSEPH HOWE began his campaign for Responsible Government, so between February and April 1839 a whole new strategy for reform began to emerge in the Canadas. On the surface it would be seen as the battle for Responsible Government. But taken even in its narrowest sense Responsible Government was half of the democratic equation. And the reform movement in the Canadas was quickly developing into a broader intellectual idea. That idea would become the basis for modern Canada.

As for British assumptions – which included Durham and his Report – they went as follows. The French Canadians would be reduced to a permanent and powerless minority through the fusing of Lower and Upper Canada. They would be further neutralized by the removal of their language from official useage. And so it didn't really matter if you were for Responsible Government or against it or somewhere in between. The new majority of *real* British subjects would think of themselves as of British race first and as reformers second. And race was what mattered.

But what if none of this were true? What if the various sorts of reformers no longer thought of themselves as either Whigs or as British first? What if they no longer believed in the old Tory–Whig opposition?

Even the older generation of William Warren Baldwin and Louis-Joseph Papineau was gradually abandoning Whig logic. After 1837 Papineau and a few others would try to relaunch themselves with Parisian ideas of revolution, equally inapplicable here. Other anglophones and franco-phones would turn to American republicanism.

Yet all of them had failed to ask the right question. What would happen if a majority of francophones and anglophones consciously thought of themselves as being from here, not there? Being from here meant that a quite different political philosophy could somehow emerge. What if these francophones and anglophones decided to work together to develop such a political philosophy? The British, the compacts, the Tories and even the dwindling group of Whigs would not see this coming because of their belief that politics was all about race, religion, language and the division of the public spoils – patronage, contracts, land.

Francophone and anglophone reformers had been repeatedly humiliated in the 1830s each time they had insisted on their British constitutional rights. What they had slowly concluded was that British constitutional rights were actually English constitutional rights, designed for Englishmen in England. What is more, apart from not living in England, most Anglo Canadians were actually Scottish, Irish, Germanic, black or from the United States, to say nothing of the francophones, to say nothing of the large number of First Nations people who voted in elections and the far larger number of First Nations who still outnumbered the newcomers and lived outside the colonial borders.

ON APRIL 12, 1839, Francis Hincks wrote a letter from the Toronto offices of *The Examiner* to Louis-Hippolyte LaFontaine. All mail went by ship, along the shore of Lake Ontario, past Kingston, through the Thousand Islands, past the Ottawa River, through the Lachine canal system to Montreal.

"The British party ... calculates as does Lord Durham on the French Canadian party being destroyed in the United

Legislature. [B]ut if we combine *as Canadians* to promote the good of all classes in Canada, there cannot be a doubt that under the new constitution" only the compacts will suffer.

This was the first of a dozen or so letters between them. LaFontaine made it clear he rejected everything in the new constitution of the amalgamated provinces designed to destroy French Canada – the loss of the French language, the denial of the francophone majority, the dumping of Upper Canada's debt onto Lower Canadians, the social and economic damage done to Lower Canada by the ongoing martial law. What slowly emerged as the letters went back and forth was their agreement that the only way around these injustices was to use the system against those who had conceived it – the English government and the local compacts.

Hincks, a close friend of the Baldwins, knew he had to draw Robert into this process. In all probability he was already in, but his mind was still on Eliza. In early 1840 he drew up his will. He was thirty-six. "[I]t is my desire that my body may be deposited in the family vault of Spadina, on the right-hand side of the remains of my dear and beloved Eliza, with whom the Almighty, praised be his holy name forever, was pleased to permit me to enjoy here a short married life of a most perfect and unbounded mutual confidence and affection and with whose blessed spirit I hope (by his Grace) to dwell in endless happiness here after."

In the midst of LaFontaine's exchange with Hincks, the new Governor General arrived and settled into Montreal. He would soon be ennobled as Lord Sydenham. His instructions from Lord John Russell, the minister of colonies, were simple: do not accept Responsible Government.

Joseph Howe immediately began attacking Russell. In October these attacks were gathered together into a book of four essays and published. It was read all over the Canadas. The Baldwins, Hincks and their allies began travelling the colony holding Responsible Government rallies. The Orange Order disrupted them. In November William Warren Baldwin and Hincks travelled in a carriage up Yonge Street to what is now Finch Avenue to speak at one of those big outdoor meetings. They arrived to find the sheriff – William Jarvis – had got there first, with whisky, clubs, other weapons and a crowd of Orange thugs. The result was a riot. A young man from the pacifist Brothers of Peace was beaten to death. Hincks was almost fatally stabbed but managed to get away. William Warren was saved by his age, but he never forgot the incident. His loathing of the Compact and the Orange Order began to grow. In the midst of this, John Strachan was installed as the first Anglican bishop of Upper Canada and set off on a province-wide tour of his parishes. This tour would in good part be about preaching the anti-democratic word.

SYDENHAM, LIKE DURHAM, could see only a derivative colonial culture. They were intellectually and emotionally unable to recognize the strong current of localness at play.

There were enormous differences of language, religion and culture within that Canadianness, but there was also an expression of place and attachment. Out of that sense of place came a shared idea of egalitarianism, natural to their life in the Americas, which would become the philosophical core of the united reform movement. What followed for reformers was a simple political necessity. If they could control the legislature across linguistic lines, they could force the acceptance of Responsible Government. That control required a complex multi-part agreement. First it was dependent on LaFontaine's ability to keep the francophone vote united to produce a strong majority in Lower Canada. Second, Baldwin would need to win at least a solid minority in the more fractious reality of Upper Canada. But third, in return for the francophone majority, he would also have to commit his MPs to support francophone rights – those basic linguistic and cultural rights that anglophones took for granted. As the historian Éric Bédard points out, LaFontaine was only able to gain the confidence of the people because he defended their language. I would add that this defence was given the force of disinterested intellect and ethics in good part because Baldwin and a slowly increasing number of his friends stood as firm on this issue as any francophone.

In other words, the reform movement was not about playing up or downplaying the importance of language and culture, or indeed any of the differences between communities. The reform movement would create a new framework for power – a framework shaped by shared ideas rather than the European/English, even U.S., concept of a *natural* unity.

And it is precisely that difference of framework that continues to make Canadians and non-Canadians uncomfortable about this country. The history of the modern Western nation-state is built on three founding monolithic mythologies: race and language and mythology itself. After the murderous disasters of the twentieth century, the race element has been happily downplayed, but it is still there as an unspoken assumption. In this model a real nation-state comprises these three elements and must have a singular face. The very idea of a nation-state intentionally built on ideas and a multiplicity of races, languages and myths doesn't fit into the historic Western framework and therefore cannot be real.

AND YET WHAT BEGAN TO EMERGE in April 1839 was exactly that alternative model. In truth the reformers were probably in a minority in both Canadas. It would take years to build between the two Canadas the trust necessary for such a movement. The anglophones would have to believe that such a broad coalition of francophones was not too broad to support reform. And the francophones would have to believe that the anglophones would support their fragile rights, even in tough times. The key to making all of this work was the development of shared ideas.

So the question was not whether they could achieve Responsible Government, but whether they could imagine and deliver the sort of society that could make Responsible Government mean something. The society they sought would therefore be intentional, not accidental or reactive.

Years later at that famous farewell banquet in Montreal in October 1851, LaFontaine, the outgoing prime minister, had to remind everyone that in the 1830s "we had a government on which parliament had no influence, it was the government you could find in all English colonies." And that is the central point: it is hard to invent systems. People know all about the various European-derived systems – the monarchies versus the republics; the imperial dictatorships versus the imperial democracies; the class-struggle societies. The colonies of these empires might have assemblies or not, but that was a secondary matter. Colonies are meant to express the imperial system and to feed wealth to the metropoles. They therefore require a colonial oligarchy to facilitate that transfer while carving off a percentage for themselves.

And so the oligarchs of the Family Compact and the Château Clique had to believe that loyalty referred to the existing system. The only other possibility was republicanism as in France or the United States. And to espouse republicanism in a monarchy was not only disloyal, it was treason. As for the ministers, MPs, soldiers and civil servants in England, they could imagine loyalty only in the context of the empire as applied from behind the mask of the Crown.

But there had to be another way. The structure of that way would be Responsible Government. And the purpose and the content would somehow have to be indigenous to this society.

THE REFORMERS KEPT WRITING to one another, developing their theory of co-operation. Hincks still seemed to be driving the process. LaFontaine was playing his hand carefully. Morin was becoming involved, as was Baldwin, quietly behind the scenes.

In February 1840 the union of the two Canadas was proclaimed, and Baldwin went into the government of Upper

Canada – now legally called Canada West – as solicitor general. A few weeks later LaFontaine refused the same offer for Canada East. He couldn't possibly have accepted. None of the wrongs done to French Canada had been righted. Had Baldwin made a mistake in accepting?

The Governor General thought he had trapped Baldwin by sucking him into serving the old system. LaFontaine thought it was a mistake. Baldwin himself wasn't sure. There was no solid reform party in Upper Canada. He had to create one. By accepting this apolitical position he was hoping to demonstrate goodwill to the moderates. And he was getting the lay of the land for the struggle ahead.

Meanwhile, LaFontaine was preparing for the next election, travelling through Lower Canada, holding public and private meetings, converting the fully justified anger and pessimism of the people and their leaders into the positive energy needed for this new battle.

On July 23 LaFontaine seems to have gone briefly to Toronto, and Hincks in September to Montreal. Such trips were common. The lake ships were large and comfortable. It took two days, and for men travelling in small groups the time spent together on board was an established part of friendship and work, the way today people spend weekends together or go to restaurants. We know little about these political trips, but the negotiations suddenly reached a pre-liminary conclusion.

On August 25 LaFontaine published his "Address to the Electors of Terrebonne" in *L'Aurore des Canadas*. This would become the political and philosophical manifesto of the reform movement. By the middle of September, Hincks had translated and published it in *The Examiner*. The result was electric in both Canadas. On November 26 Baldwin replied to one of LaFontaine's letters with what amounted to his own equivalent of "The Electors of Terrebonne." LaFontaine wrote back with a cool, severe reminder that the Lower Canadians had been given no choice over the union, as their constitution and legislature were still suspended. But the Upper Canadian MPs "have assumed the responsibility of the Union Bill by passing it. If they have been deceived in their expectations they must protest...." If they didn't there would be a terrible break between anglophones and franco-phones. "They, as well as ourselves, would have to suffer from the internal divisions.... And yet theirs and ours is a common cause. It is the interest of both Provinces to meet on the field in the legislature in a spirit of peace, of union, of friendship and of fraternity. Unity of purpose is more nec-essary now than ever. I entertain no doubt that the Reformers of Upper Canada feel this necessity as deeply as ourselves, and that in the first Session of the Legislature they will give us unequivocal proofs of that feeling, as a pledge of mutual and enduring confidence."

Baldwin replied that "the Reformers of Upper Canada ... are resolved to unite with their Lower Canadian Brethren cordially as friends, and to afford them every assistance in obtaining justice, *upon precisely the same footing in every particular as ourselves.*"

LaFontaine's "Address" was a great deal more than a simple political statement. In it he called for the end of seigneurial rights. "We must employ all the means in our power to equalize the ranks of society, to wrest from Government all hope of establishing in this country an aristocratic power centre, however small." He argued for a St. Lawrence Seaway. He called for public schooling. "Education is the primary blessing which Government can confer upon a people." He presented a still-modern view of immigration. "Canada is the land of our ancestors; it is our country as it must be the adopted country of the various populations which come from diverse portions of the Globe. Like us their paramount desire must be the happiness and prosperity of Canada, as the heritage which they should endeavour to transmit to their descendants.... Above all, their children must be like ourselves CANADIANS." Of course, he made the argument for Responsible Government and warned that it would be difficult to get. But it was essential because it was a matter of "political liberty," and the popular will must control the adoption of laws, taxes and the machinery of government.

But the core argument running through his "Address" was that this new alliance of francophones and anglophones, this new political strategy, this new framework for imagining their future, was all about egalitarianism. "We will secure to ourselves political liberty, the enjoyment whereof we cannot be debarred from so long as social equality continues to be as it now is, the characteristic feature of the population as well of Upper Canada as of Lower Canada. For that equality must necessarily lead to political liberty, towards the attainment of which an irresistible tendency exists in the British Colonies of North America. The habits of a people are stronger than the laws imposed upon it.... No privileged caste, beyond and above the mass of the people, can exist in Canada."

This is the basis upon which Canada became a democracy. It was from the 1840s on the central theme of the democratic movement created by LaFontaine and Baldwin, leading directly to contemporary Canada. And this "Address to the Electors of Terrebonne" is the key founding statement of what we understand Canada to be.

CHAPTER FIVE

Discovering Friendship

It would be seven years before they won their battle. Progress was followed by failure and retreat, elections were won and lost. The Reformers committed errors both comic and tragic while making brilliant breakthroughs. There were betrayals by close friends, who would later wander back into the Reform camp. Only at a distance could the cause be seen to be slowly advancing.

In the end LaFontaine and Baldwin became, each in his own way, clever and ruthless politicians. But by the time victory came, they were almost too worn down by the effort to sustain themselves in office.

Their seven years would begin in Kingston because Lord Sydenham had chosen that small Lake Ontario city as the capital. It was a beautiful, even dramatic, spot at the southern entrance of the Rideau Canal and source of the St. Lawrence River.

Sydenham had rented for himself a large neoclassical mansion, Alwington House, on a bay just outside town with a view of islands and lake. The new city hospital, right on the edge of Kingston and still standing today, had been gutted and rebuilt as the Parliament, to house the Legislative Assembly and the Legislative Council. Money was liberally spent to create British-style gathering places – wood panelling, large red leather chairs, swaths of heavy curtains.

Kingston had been a First Nations settlement, then a French trading and military headquarters, then densely Loyalist. By 1841 it was heavily Irish Protestant, an Orange Order centre, economically stagnant with almost no public infrastructure or services. This circumstance mattered because the government came with several thousand public servants. To summarize the situation: the sewage flowed into a bay just about where the drinking water came out. And so gastroenteritis was a central feature of setting up the new Canada.

Sydenham chose Kingston precisely because it was anglophone, pro-British and Protestant. Canada was to become like England: unilingual and anti-Catholic.

It is hard today to recreate the pretensions of these imperial governors and the structure of class and superiority with which they governed. Sydenham was a good administrator, but he was also a particularly egotistical English politician. He probably wasn't capable of admitting, even to himself, his most undebatable weakness – fairly advanced syphilis. He made up for it by using the aura of his vice-regal position to get into the bed of every possible woman, virginal, married, whatever.

Sydenham's idea of himself was a logical expression of London's idea of itself. In both cases, the solution to the rebellions was to make Canada English and loyal. This pretension was European culture's destiny. Non-Europeans – colonials – were to bend to its superiority. How well this approach went during Kingston's four years as the capital of Canada can be seen in the fate of three successive Governors General. One after the other, they grew sick and died, as if a deeply ironic God had cast a curse on the idea of a unilingual, Protestant capital for a country that was neither. In fact, if you believed in an active, vengeful God, which the Family Compact, the Anglican bishop John Strachan, the Methodist pope Egerton Ryerson and the Orange Order all did, you would have to conclude that he wasn't on your side.

The Reformers did not like Kingston. Baldwin called it an "Orange hole." They found the racial and religious tensions unbearable. Perhaps because of these fault lines, it was there that LaFontaine and Baldwin discovered they could work together. More important, they discovered that they could become friends. This intimacy was not something for which either of them had a talent. They were not easy, outgoing men. LaFontaine had his wife and one friend, Joseph-Amable Berthelot. Baldwin had no friends outside his family. They would gradually become each other's closest friend.

IT BEGAN WITH the election of March 1841, the first of the newly unified Canada. Given Sydenham's instructions from London and his temperament, he needed to win. And so he climbed down off his throne, abandoning all pretense of neutrality, and threw himself into the details of electoral politics. He wanted to defeat the Reformers without falling into the hands of the compacts. He brought in from London an expert in election manipulation, then set about gerrymandering ridings, particularly in Lower Canada, to maximize the effect of the anglophone vote. He organized violent gangs to take over the hustings platforms upon which you had to vote. They would club any Reformer who tried to climb up. According to Michael Cross, violence was decisive in seventeen out of eighty-four ridings, and four people were killed in Upper Canada, four in Lower Canada. Sydenham carefully named the election officer in each riding to ensure the gangs had free sway. The governor was attempting to create and elect his personal political party.

He might have got away with all of this, but his ego drove him one step too far. He had never forgiven LaFontaine for his refusal to accept office earlier in the year. And so he focused on the destruction of Lower Canada's leader by defeating him in his own riding. But virtually everyone in the Terrebonne riding just north of Montreal, including most anglophones, would vote Reform. LaFontaine arrived on the morning of March 20 to mobilize his supporters. He had already distributed his "Address," attacking the forced union of the two colonies as "an act of injustice and of despotism." He added that Responsible Government could rectify this evil by producing "good, constitutional and effective government…. The Reformers in the two provinces form an immense majority…. Our cause is common." Supporters of his opponent, an Irish Protestant doctor, had been threatening people in Terrebonne for a month. The hustings platform had been intentionally placed at the far end of the riding, a good ten kilometres away from where most people lived. Sleighloads of Protestant road workers – stone crushers – as well as an Upper Canadian militia group out of uniform rushed across the riding, waving clubs and shouting insults.

On the morning of the twenty-second, a Monday, at seven o'clock, LaFontaine began walking at the head of seven hundred voters the ten kilometres to New Glasgow, a tiny village in which the hustings platform had been built. Many carried clubs, more joined them along the way. The last kilometre followed a track along the bottom of a valley with hundreds of armed men taunting them from the snow-covered hills on either side. Fighting began to break out on the edges, and blood could be seen spreading here and there on the white ground. It became apparent that many of the thugs also carried rifles.

And so there he was, a young man of thirty-four with a history of physically throwing himself into riots. Now he stood, as the cliché goes, at the crossroads of history. He was the leader of French Canada. Baldwin insisted on treating LaFontaine as the leader of all Reformers. If he led his voters the last hundred metres up the hill to the schoolhouse where the hustings stood, surrounded by these imported gangs, there would be deaths, perhaps a massacre. And even if his people managed to take control of the hustings platform long enough to vote and win, he would still lose. He would have allowed himself to be taunted into descending onto the old European terrain of hatred and violence between races and religions. He would have betrayed his principle of citizenship and of the middle way. Sydenham would probably claim that the French Canadians were reverting to rebellion. He might use this as an excuse once again to limit their rights.

Restraint! This was one of those moments, both real and mythological, when the leader of the democratic movement understood that the true nature of Canada, if it were to exist, lay in restraint and the acceptance of complexity.

Calmly, at least on the outside, LaFontaine withdrew his candidacy and set about persuading his followers to walk away. It was a victory that looked and felt like a defeat – one of those revolutionary political breakthroughs that produced a theory later attributed to people like Tolstoy and Gandhi.

A week later LaFontaine published a detailed description of what had happened, including a verbal attack on Sydenham and an announcement. "I am withdrawing from public life; I go back to private life with no desire to leave it." His bitterness and anger had every reason to be real. He had played by the rules of English democracy and been met with the lowest form of thuggery from those same English.

BY EARLY MAY he had digested his anger and was back in the game.

The Governor General was still running things from Montreal, having not yet moved up to the new capital.

Baldwin was in town. Theoretically he had come to Montreal to be sworn in to the new government. In reality, everything he did destabilized that government. He wrote to the Governor General and to the ministers already in place to tell them that while he might become their colleague, he had no confidence in them. What's more, if asked in the House he would be obliged, as an honourable man, to admit as much. That raised the unasked question, How could the House vote confidence in a government if its own ministers had no confidence in one another? Then he went to Government House to be sworn in but refused a key part of that ceremony, the Oath of Supremacy – the legal supremacy of the English Anglican Church over the Roman Church. Baldwin pointed out that the Pope already had a role in Canada through the formalized religious rights of French Canada, going back to the cession of Canada by the French King to the English King. Therefore, the Anglican Church was not supreme here. Therefore the oath could not be sworn to. Whether Baldwin had a plan or not, he was engaged in experimental guerrilla warfare, demonstrating from within what was wrong with the system.

Why did Sydenham put up with all of this? Because he needed Baldwin. Because, despite extreme efforts, his personal conservative party had won only twenty-four of the eighty-four seats. Even under the gerrymandered system, LaFontaine had won twenty. There were up to twenty-five anglophone Reformers, even though Baldwin had little control over their votes.

Meanwhile, Baldwin was meeting, dining, walking, planning with the Montreal Reformers. Given the ambiguous election results, there was great latitude for advancing the Reform program. The cabinet was dominated by mere courtiers and technicians, including the de facto prime minister, William Henry Draper, a smooth, agreeable, relatively effective man. He served others and did his best within the rules.

After a few days Sydenham allowed as how the Oath of Supremacy was not legally essential. So Baldwin did join the cabinet, really as internal opposition. And he continued to spend most of his time with LaFontaine.

In early June MPs steamed up or down to the new capital of Kingston and made their way from farming areas over dirt paths and the odd corduroy road by horse or carriage. Parliament was to open on the fourteenth. Baldwin had advisers like Francis Hincks and Augustin-Norbert Morin. But the key man, LaFontaine, waited quietly in Montreal. On the tenth, Baldwin went to Alwington House to insist that Sydenham name francophone ministers to the cabinet.

Without them the government was not real and he might have to resign.

Three days later Sydenham wrote to fire him – or rather to accept the resignation he had not quite offered. It really doesn't matter which, because this quickly revealed itself as a historic moment. It demonstrated that the Reform movement could not be bought in the old colonial way because it was about principles first and power second. And it showed that the anglophones would stand with the francophones, even if it cost them power.

Baldwin had been thrown out the day before Parliament opened. And this opening was in itself historic, being the first time in the history of empire that a colonial assembly had come together with the expectation that it could and would instruct the government.

Joseph Howe had travelled up from Halifax to be there. He was now the Speaker of the Nova Scotia Assembly and so had been seated in a place of honour, inside the bar of the upper House.

Almost immediately the groups began manoeuvring, first over the election of the Speaker. It would show who controlled the legislature. Sir Allan MacNab was running in order to demonstrate that loyal men should be in charge. Baldwin persuaded the nascent Reform Party to put forward

Augustin Cuvillier, a moderate, fully bilingual francophone and a Catholic. This was not the world London had gone to so much trouble to create. But Cuvillier clearly had the numbers. Draper embraced his candidacy to make it unanimous – that is, to make it seem as if the Reformers had exercised no power over the government and the governor. So Francis Hincks jumped up and said he supported Cuvillier only because of the candidate's "entire want of confidence in the present administration." His election would therefore represent the House's lack of confidence. Pandemonium followed. Someone asked Cuvillier if this was so. He cleverly refused to answer, suggesting that it could be so, but to say that would be inappropriate. He was then elected. It was a small Reform victory.

Seven years of this sort of manoeuvring lay ahead. Almost immediately Baldwin engaged Draper in a courtroom-like cross-examination as to when and why he might resign. Would he step down if he did not have the confidence of the House? In other words, was he Sydenham's creature or a servant of the people's elected representatives? To question after question Draper bobbed and weaved. He was a smooth performer. Through seven speeches he managed to obfuscate until finally Baldwin cornered him, and Draper had no choice if he wished to win any House votes in the future. He allowed as how he would resign if he lost the House's confidence. It was another Reform victory.

But over the months that followed Sydenham used his patronage powers, buying off one member after another. And he had deep pockets. His first great victory came when Francis Hincks, ever the businessman and believer in economic progress, began to vote with the government. It was an almost unbearable betrayal, coming from the man who had put LaFontaine and Baldwin together. He was a smart man with good intentions but had no ethical compass. He simply couldn't understand that *economic progress* was Sydenham's strategy to prove that Canada could have reform without democracy and without the French Canadians. Baldwin responded with absolute support for Lower Canada's positions. He had to demonstrate his loyalty to their shared cause. But many of the anglophone Reformers, used to the old, corrupt ways, rose to the governor's temptations and began to drift off. It looked as if Sydenham might win by breaking up the movement.

Then, quite unexpectedly, three things happened almost at once. The first came out of Baldwin's imagination. In those days you could run for election in two ridings. It was a safety feature, particularly for leaders. If you won in both, you had to choose one, and there would be a by-election in the other. Baldwin had won in Hastings, near Belleville, and in the North Riding of York, north of Toronto running up to Lake Simcoe. The plan had been for William Warren to run in the by-election.

Baldwin wrote to his father on August 10, asking him to step aside in favour of LaFontaine. The gesture would create an electrical storm of the political sort across both Canadas: the francophone leader – until recently under arrest as a rebel, back from exile only three years before, once a close adviser to Papineau – would run in a rural, Protestant, Upper Canadian riding. The two men had vowed there must be no question of race. This candidacy would prove it was possible. LaFontaine would be the first francophone most of the voters had met. He came from another world, days away by ship, farther away than London from Paris, eleven hours of travel from Toronto by coach over mud roads.

Baldwin didn't ask for LaFontaine's approval. He wanted first to make sure this improbable scheme would work. William Warren understood the implications immediately: "It will have a most happy influence on the politics of the United Province." And he went to work. Within five days the Reform riding president summarized the situation: "As justice has been refused to the Lower Canadians [I] will support Mr. L."

Baldwin wrote to LaFontaine on the fifteenth, admitting what he had done. Four days later LaFontaine replied, clearly moved. "My sincere thanks for the mark of confidence in my political principles."

But all of this was about more than politics. It was over those few weeks from mid-August to mid-September that they consciously realized they could trust each other, that they began to become each other's closest friend.

But why North York? It had been William Lyon Mackenzie's seat. And then Robert Baldwin's. It was a Reform seat in good part because of a large, rich, breakaway Quaker community around the village of Hope at Sharon. They called themselves the Children of Peace and were led by David Willson. There, in the 1820s, they built perhaps the most spiritual building in Canada, the Sharon Temple, a wooden meeting hall of three elegant squares rising from largest to smallest as if shrinking by some magical proportion, light and airy, every architectural element in it, no matter how minute, symbolic of their beliefs. It still has all of its magical qualities. I once spoke at the modest podium and was overwhelmed with the palpable living sense that Mackenzie, LaFontaine and both Baldwins had changed our idea of the public good from that spot.

The Children of Peace had created the first Canadian

agricultural co-operative and then the first public co-operative bank. They were deeply committed to an egalitarian, democratic society. Still, their votes alone would not be enough. Baldwin published an address to the electors: "The return of Mr. LaFontaine by an Upper Canadian constituency will be a substantial pledge of our sympathy with our Lower Canada friends and form the strongest band of union between us." At the same time he was fretting in private and funding the campaign. To his father: "Let it be what it may, he must not be defeated."

By late August LaFontaine was in Kingston, planning with Baldwin, who could not leave the city if they were to hold the Reform MPs together. Then he sailed on with Étienne Parent to Toronto.

William Warren was on the dock to greet him and was at his enthusiastic, humanist, all-embracing best. LaFontaine had finally found a father figure with whom he could have a warm, supportive two-way relationship. The idea was that he would stay with the Baldwin family on Front Street. At first Phoebe was resistant, convinced that she wasn't up to "Montreal Gentlemen [who] are so accustomed to style." He would be unhappy. She was quite wrong. LaFontaine immediately became part of the family, surrounded by the children and the children's friends. This was the home life he had always wanted. They all doted on him and he on them.

The eldest daughter, Maria, reported to her father in Kingston. "Mr. LaFontaine arrived yesterday and has been with us ever since. I have taken it into my head that his manners are like yours." A week later she added, "The more I see of Mr. LaFontaine the more I think him like you in his manners and indeed so everyone in the house says."

It was as if LaFontaine had always been there, an uncle or a godfather. And this atmosphere solidified another of Baldwin's ideas – that the children should go to school in French. They would make up for their father's lack of language skills by becoming bilingual and symbols of the future. Baldwin was right. His children did become symbols of the loyalty of Upper Canadian Reformers to Lower Canadians. That was perhaps not the most humane way to think of childhood, but the two girls and Robert, the youngest, did particularly well out of it. And Maria would go on to play a key role in the politics of the Reform movement.

A week later, LaFontaine and William Warren set off early in the morning by carriage through heavy mud. It took twelve hours to get to the York riding. They arrived in darkness to find the Sharon Temple illuminated with hundreds of candles for an annual gathering. The effect was otherworldly. LaFontaine was thrown into the strange environment of Protestant rural Ontario. Day after day of inns, supporters' houses, endless meetings. The women were far more present than in the cities, with Quaker women coming to political meetings. William Warren would warm up the crowd, then LaFontaine would take the floor, with his solid but heavily accented English. And as the father reported to his son, the farmers would cheer this rare bird from Montreal.

On the same day that his father and friend had set off to campaign, Robert Baldwin in Kingston unexpectedly rose in the legislature to introduce four resolutions calling for Responsible Government. These constituted the Reform Party's parliamentary manifesto. It was September 3, 1841, and this was the second of the three events to change the country's direction.

In fact, Baldwin had already quietly negotiated four somewhat different resolutions with Draper's government and therefore with Sydenham. This deal had involved compromise and so the resolutions were much weakened. But before the minister responsible could introduce them, Baldwin jumped up with his own original version, breaking their agreement. Anger and accusations of betrayal followed. Eventually the government introduced their weaker version.

In order to defeat Baldwin's resolutions they had to argue that theirs were just as strong, perhaps stronger. At that point the Reformers rallied around and accepted them. It had been a devious but clever manoeuvre, and as Michael Cross has put it, the myth was thus born of a great victory for Baldwin and for Responsible Government. Many would feel years later that this had been his greatest moment. He had forced the Governor General's men to defend what they opposed – a Parliament-led democracy.

The next day, Saturday, September 4, came the third unexpected event. Lord Sydenham was riding home from a tryst. He was thrown by his horse, but one foot caught in the stirrup and he was dragged along, upside down, dirt being ground into a bad leg wound. Within a few days he had tetanus. His health was already undermined by syphilis, and now lockjaw set in. He could neither speak nor eat. Within two weeks he was dead. It was September 19, 1841.

LaFontaine was elected by an overwhelming majority on the twenty-third.

Parliament was prorogued in time for a massive state funeral in St. George's Cathedral. Kingston had never seen anything like it. Some historians have tried to emphasize Sydenham's administrative reforms and other specific good initiatives. But the reality is that he had set out to destroy our growing democratic system, caused the death of dozens of people and treated the citizenry with contempt.

Now the greatest force began to assert itself. Winter. The MPs scattered, making their way home before Lake Ontario became too rough and then froze over. Baldwin was back where he always preferred to be, in the midst of his family, every available generation dining together in the big house on Front Street. Eliza's shrine sat waiting for him upstairs behind a locked door, an oasis of peace, filled with every one of her beloved objects. In Montreal, LaFontaine and Adèle adopted a young girl of nine, his niece, Corinne Weilbrenner. He would later write to Baldwin that she had changed the meaning of their lives.

CHAPTER SIX

Surviving Politics

An empire rarely changes its mind simply because it fails. It is driven by a larger sense of its own destiny, no matter how stupid that is. And so early in January 1843, Sir Charles Bagot, the new Governor General, arrived in Kingston by sleigh across the Lake Ontario ice.

An intelligent man, not an egomaniac like Sydenham, a highly successful diplomat, he nevertheless arrived with exactly the same instructions from the same sort of imperial politicians who might have believed in democracy and citizenship at home but not in the colonies: "[Y]ou will endeavour to avail yourself of the advice and services of the ablest men, without reference to party distinctions, which, upon every occasion, you will do your utmost to discourage." What the colonial secretary meant was that Bagot should ignore ideas, beliefs and ethical parameters and simply administer on the basis of particular interests.

So the Governor General set out with charm to divide and conquer. He was bilingual but in private dismissed its relevance here. He made good appointments, travelled, reached out. His weapon was that of all governors – patronage. Buy them off to win them over.

In the autumn the MPs returned, and it became clear before Parliament opened that Draper's government couldn't win a vote in the House. There was no confidence. Responsible Government would not go away. Even Draper advised Bagot to bring in the Reformers. He himself would not serve with them, certainly not with Baldwin, who was detested by the establishment for his ethical rigour.

Bagot tried everything. He called in LaFontaine and offered him power without Baldwin. He offered a great deal to the francophones "as a Race, as a people rather than as a Party." He needed to put a wedge between the two men. Hincks was enticed to take the chief financial role, but then he was easy to tempt. What Bagot needed was for the French Canadians to come in as a race and thus neutralize both themselves and the Upper Canadian democrats. He reassured London: "There is hardly any extremity to which I should not be disposed to submit or hazard which I might not think it even prudent to incur, rather than see Mr. Baldwin again introduced into the Council." But LaFontaine simply said no to every offer. He and Baldwin had carefully talked through these issues. Language, religion, cultural particularities all existed and mattered. But their Reform Party – their organized expression of principles and ideas – was the only hope.

Bagot was amazed. His last desperate manoeuvre was to reveal to the freshly assembled Parliament every detail of his negotiations. The revelation of looming French power as well as general Reform inflexibility was supposed to terrify all the moderates into line. LaFontaine therefore rose from his front-row Opposition seat to explain himself in a firm but unterrifying way. This was the first time most of the Upper Canadian members had ever seen him in the flesh. To anglophones LaFontaine was either the romantic, courageous leader described by Baldwin or the dangerous rebel conjured up by the government.

"Si je me lève en ce moment, M. l'Orateur ..."

And then, in one of those astonishing moments of self-immolation, Mr. Dunn, a cabinet minister, shouted out that LaFontaine should speak English. As he let loose these words, the whole idea that the Governor General and the old school could go on governing for everyone seemed to evaporate forever.

LaFontaine gazed over at Mr. Dunn, paused, then with the dispassionate, elegant, cool tone for which he was becoming famous, continued in French. He thanked Mr. Dunn "car

le fait que cette demande vient d'un des membres du cabinet"
demonstrated why the House had no confidence in the government. When he had finished, Baldwin jumped up and in
a rare angry, funny, patriotic harangue destroyed what
remained of Draper's authority and the imperial government's pretension that it could govern from afar. He reminded everyone of the evil done to francophones from 1837 to
1841. And then ... "I was an advocate for the union of the
two Provinces and still am, but not for a union of parchment,
but for the union of hearts of free born men. Not a union
forced down the throats of the people by bayonets, but
a union of the voluntary choice of a free people. I am a
Canadian born, son of a Canadian, the grandson of a man
who made Canada his home."

He picked apart the government's policies, mocked them,
the House laughing along with him. "Any man who would
vote confidence in [such a] ministry ... should be sent to a
Lunatic Asylum." Then he reintroduced the Responsible
Government resolutions in a much strengthened form. And
LaFontaine was back on his feet.

By the end of the day, Draper's government was dead. It
would not win a vote of confidence. Bagot was left with two
choices: rule by fiat or give in. It took another three days of
negotiation before Bagot collapsed, and on September 16,

1842, LaFontaine was named de facto prime minister. This was the first Responsible Government – democratic government – in any colony in imperial history, any imperial history. And the prime minister was a francophone Catholic. The Governor General was a fine diplomat, so he immediately reframed his defeat as a victory. "This great measure," he called it, in an attempt to capture the mythological opportunity to be seen as the man who made it all possible.

He eventually received great credit in Canada for two reasons. First, because the political leaders in London condemned what had happened, Whigs and Tories alike: Sir Robert Peel, Lord Stanley, Ewart Gladstone, Lord John Russell. The Duke of Wellington said, "What a fool the man must have been, to act as he has done." They were all horrified. It is a reminder that throughout our colonial history the great leaders of England, whether Whig or Tory, Liberal or Conservative, including all the great democratic reformers, were unanimously against democracy in Lower and Upper Canada, and in Nova Scotia, the petri dishes of imperial experiments.

Bagot had arrived with a weak heart. All of this rejection from London and anger from the Canadian Tories was too much for him, and his health began to collapse. Still, he had succeeded in placing himself as a Canadian mythological hero. But as Michael Cross points out, Bagot was not the hero, real or mythological, of Responsible Government. He was defeated by LaFontaine and Baldwin. The Reformers went along with his self-aggrandizement because his new-found enthusiasm isolated the Tories and gave the new government legitimacy. That is the second reason he got such credit. The only heroes were the Reformers.

For the next six months, Canada was effortlessly governed by its democratic government. They were more than competent. Parliament functioned and there was a public sense of progress. As Bagot's heart disease gradually sidelined him, the prime minister and Baldwin were increasingly in charge, and the country grew accustomed to a real government.

Not that the two friends' problems went away. LaFontaine's inflammatory rheumatism struck him the moment he was sworn in, and he was confined to bed for several weeks in unbearable pain. On taking office, ministers in that time had to run for re-election. LaFontaine won easily in North York, but Baldwin faced the full anger of the Orangemen and the Compact in Hastings. It turned into the most violent by-election Canada had seen.

Baldwin to LaFontaine, October 6, 1842: "The troops are here and I really believe if they had not come we should have had hard work here tonight…. I of course do not desire any interference that would be inconsistent with principle."

LaFontaine to Baldwin, October 7: "I hope there will be no necessity for the Returning officer to use the active assistance of the Military – for God's sake, let him, by all means, avoid it, if he can. I need not say how much I feel for you – Have patience and courage – If you are not returned, many of the Lower Canada members will offer you a seat."

And so Baldwin ended up running in Rimouski, well up the St. Lawrence on the south side. There his election committee understood they were making history. "[C]ela fournit un occasion au Bas-Canada ..." This gives Lower Canada a chance to render to Upper Canada the same compliment paid when Monsieur LaFontaine was defeated by violence in Terrebonne.... Violence has now defeated Mr. Baldwin. [He] gave to us unequivocal proof that he is incapable of sacrificing his principles to his individual interest."

He was easily elected and both men settled into governing. Adèle LaFontaine moved to Kingston. Baldwin's children visited whenever they could. In the spring of 1843 Maria Baldwin was taken down to Quebec City to begin school with the Ursulines. Many of the Lower Canadian MPs went on to Toronto to call on William Warren, now the old sage. LaFontaine himself would sometimes turn up unexpectedly on Front Street, surprise the old man and see the remaining children. Eventually they also went off to school in Quebec City, where they became an excuse or a pleasant reason for political leaders to visit or to deliver them home to Toronto or back to school. If the legislature wasn't sitting, the children would pause on the way to stay with the LaFontaines in Montreal. Baldwin himself particularly liked Quebec City and chaperoned them one way or the other whenever he could. All these visits were as political as they were familial. In fact, the leading politicians took to travelling back and forth to the cities between Toronto and Quebec City for any number of reasons: getting to know one another, doing business together. There was a relaxed familiarity about all of this, which is often lost in the classic political story of leaders and power won or lost.

LaFontaine and Baldwin began to transform the country by moving a barrage of laws through Parliament. Perhaps most important was an election bill aimed at stopping the violence and manipulation. The number of voters doubled within three years. A public education bill focused people on the direct link between taxes and egalitarian society: if you want an educated population you have to pay taxes, an idea that infuriated the Tories. Baldwin argued with a certain ironic contempt that "surely those who are so fortunate as to belong to that favoured class, could not be so narrow-minded and so blind to their own interests, as to object to be taxed to effect this great and important object." The Lower Canadian ridings were re-established as they had been before Sydenham's gerrymandering. The House removed one particularly arbitrary power from the Governor General by voting heavily to move the capital to Montreal. They established the independence of judges, in part by banning public employees from these positions. Equally important, they began to change the face of the public service. Suddenly farmers and habitants were being named to local positions. This opening-up would eventually bring down the government under the charge that they were usurping the Governor General's right to control patronage and that they were no better than the old compacts, using power to reward friends. Of course, patronage still existed. But they were broadening the base of democracy by opening public positions up to a wide variety of people and in the process removing a major source of income from the tiny interconnected compacts. And they were laying the foundations of a professional civil service, which began with their appointment of Étienne Parent as clerk of the Executive Council – head of the civil service. He would remain in the job for over a quarter century, until after Confederation.

Both Parliament and the civil service began to act as if the law denying French its official role simply did not exist. Parliamentary debate was bilingual, but the government also moved quickly to re-establish French in both legal documents and the courts. Except in the constitution – controlled by London – French was back. The effective ban had lasted not quite three years.

News of this unprecedented form of government spread beyond Canada's borders. Both LaFontaine and Baldwin were elected vice-presidents of the International Anti-Slave Trade Movement based in Paris. The equivalent today would be one of those lists of prominent world figures standing up against global warming or the dictatorship in Burma. Their names being on such a list wasn't surprising. What they had done in a few months was remarkable, a harbinger of the international liberal movement that would come to power briefly in so many places five years later.

By March 1843 Bagot was so sick that he had to resign. He lingered on in Alwington House, bedridden, imploring the Reformers to defend his reputation as the father of *his* democratic system. Which they did. There was still every political reason to go along with his image of himself. Besides, he had come over to their side and been agreeable and supportive in every way.

LIKE BAGOT, the new Governor General, Sir Charles Metcalfe, arrived by sleigh across the ice with the same old pre-democratic instructions from London – get Canada back under control.

Alwington House had been turned into a palliative care unit, so Metcalfe rented a temporary house. He was yet another competent colonial administrator and a Whig. But British Whigs, once in Canada, fast turned into Compact-supporting Tories. He began slowly, appearing to work comfortably with his government as he tried to pull back the elements of power strand by strand. All the while, LaFontaine's government continued to do good things. The amnesties continued, and Wolfred Nelson was soon back in Canada. LaFontaine, in an almost impossible negotiation, managed to get Papineau an amnesty in 1845, but he chose to stay in Paris for another year.

The break with Metcalfe began with the Secret Societies Bill. The Orange Order ran exactly like a Bolshevik organization: at every level it met and operated in secret. It was the source of violence in Canada and would have been happy to overthrow the government by any means. Baldwin's bill set out to make organizations like this illegal. Parliament passed it with a large majority, which went well beyond the Reformers. Metcalfe refused to sign it, claiming it was "unexampled in British legislation." This was a lie. A single example: Pitt the Younger had passed the Treasonable Practices Bill; various societies were shut down, the creation of others forbidden. Metcalfe refused because the Orangemen were on his side.

In fact, the Governor General may have been right that banning them wouldn't work. Our subsequent history shows that organizations like these are best defeated by the firm application of fair laws by clear government standards and above all by public education.

Metcalfe continually expanded his power by appointing supporters to public jobs without consulting his government. It was the old patronage problem. LaFontaine and Baldwin finally stood their ground over a particular nomination, a crisis followed, and in November 1843 they resigned in protest. They did so in full confidence that this would be the final challenge to the anti-democratic system, a challenge they could easily win. In the meantime, the same old purposeless group returned to power under Draper, who managed to peel off two respected French-Canadian conservatives, Papineau's brother and old Denis-Benjamin Viger.

The Reformers began organizing with energy and enthusiasm for the historic election. But they had miscalculated.

Power lost is power gone. First Metcalfe downgraded the role of Parliament, not bothering to call it back for a year in the hope that people would forget how well democracy had worked. When finally summoned, the MPs were given little to do. Metcalfe ran an old-fashioned, quiet, unaggressive colonial dictatorship: divide and conquer with contracts and patronage, drawing the various elites back into that comfort zone of vice-regal kindness without the burdens of citizen responsibility.

In Upper Canada, where as always there were more divisions, Baldwin and his allies created the Reform Association of Canada on February 6, 1844. Baldwin launched it with one of his good speeches. "It is not by weakening, but by strengthening the influence of the people, not by enlarging but by confining within narrow limits the power of the Imperial authorities in colonial affairs, that harmony will be restored." Myriad public dinners and mass meetings followed. Soon there were twenty-two branches around the province, drawing in a whole new generation of Reformers.

This was good and bad. Led by men like George Brown, who would found the movement's best paper, *The Globe*, some of these new Reformers would gradually evolve into a quite different movement – the Clear Grits – often described as being to the left of the Reformers. Yes and no. What they sought was a European, ideological style of clarity on issues, just as the aging Papineau and his young followers would a few years later. And it is that obsession with clarity that has so often divided Canadians into apparently irreconcilable groups and created most of the serious problems in our modern history.

In any case, the Reform Association seemed to sweep Upper Canada. As part of the campaign LaFontaine and Baldwin decided to go back to running in their respective home ridings – Terrebonne and North York – to show that democracy was now normalized.

But the democratic principles they advanced were not yet understood by the majority of people. With their resignation from government they had provoked a crisis the voters didn't want. There was a sense that they should have found a way to go on governing, not pick a fight. And the political habits of corruption, religious division, patronage, violence and race-based arguments were too recent. Many moderates were not convinced that there was space in the world for Canadian-born political and philosophical initiatives that were not derivatives of those of England or France, or even of the United States. That same colonial insecurity still hangs over us.

Baldwin in particular had to struggle riding by riding,

meeting by meeting. He built the campaign around their new style of democracy, and the equally new Canadian nationalism. "I would show to the world that as Canadians we have a country and are a people.... Our cause is not that merely of a party. It is the cause of our country."

But religious leaders, like the Methodist Egerton Ryerson, worried that the new democracy was too intellectual, too focused on practical reforms, not devotional enough. He worked hard for Metcalfe, dividing the Reform vote. This was the second great mistake of his career. Ryerson more than anyone else was to blame for Canada's falling off the democratic track in 1844, losing four years at a time of relative international calm, years that might have helped us to avoid the divisions, destruction and deaths of 1849.

Put another way, each of the Reform government's initiatives would cost the movement votes: removing the capital from Kingston; the Secret Society Bill; the taxation measures; Baldwin's attempt to make universities secular. The leaders of most interest groups were already against the Reformers, but not all of their members were. Now the looming possibility of full democracy frightened them. LaFontaine couldn't help pointing out in a letter to his friend that anglophones were held back by their divisive religious sects.

Formal campaigning began in October 1844. The results by November 12 showed an anti-Reform majority – not enormous, but real. It was a victory for the old colonial model. London was delighted. Gladstone praised Metcalfe's "Administration as one which … may justly be regarded as a model by his successors." He was made a baronet for defeating democracy.

For LaFontaine and Baldwin, it was a disaster. From such hopes suddenly everything was turning sour. William Warren had faded and died early in the new year. For LaFontaine it was the end of his most successful father-figure relationship. The only letter in which Baldwin let himself go was to his friend and ally:

> While he was yet with us it seemed to me as if I grudged every moment that I was obliged to pass out of his room; and when he was gone, when he who had been the protection of my childhood, the guide of my youth and the Counsellor of my manhood was no more and I felt in all its weight the truth that I was indeed for the first time without a father I was more overwhelmed than I had expected.
>
> And you, my dear friend, will not I am sure be surprised at my feeling little able to return at

once to other subjects – and least of all to that of
politics from which if I could with honour I would
fly forever.

LaFontaine replied that it was "as if he had been one of
my parents." Toronto was virtually shut down for the funeral. René-Édouard Caron, the mayor of Quebec City, went to
the Ursulines to break the news gently to Maria.

As depressing election results dribbled in, LaFontaine's
niece and adopted daughter suddenly died. "[T]he affliction
which I experienced by the death of my little niece – Mrs. L.
has been very ill; but she is now recovering. You have children; we have not. Corinne was our adopted daughter. Her
death will, I am afraid, exercise a great influence over my
plans and calculations – I must submit." Suddenly he had
lost all his old energy and certainty of direction. "No one
feels more than I do the responsibilities that hangs on my
shoulders – I wish you had come down – I hope to see you
soon – I wish to have your advice – situated as I am, my
position has nothing to be envied. I have one consolation;
my conscience reproaches nothing."

Each of them began reporting to the other with increasing frequency how sick they were. Their physical decline had
begun after the resignation of the government, as if they

instinctively understood they had made a mistake. LaFontaine was invaded by inflammatory rheumatism, then headaches that would not go away. Baldwin was laid up with dysentery. He wrote to his friend, "You must, however, allow me still to look to you as my leader while your health permits you to remain in public life." In January 1845 Baldwin fell into a prolonged depression. It coincided with the anniversary of Eliza's death nine years before. In March he went to Montreal by coach over the terrible roads, and the coach repeatedly turned over, leaving him with strained muscles and serious bruising. In June LaFontaine wrote to him, "I feel I am growing old, for I find more pleasure in my [legal practice than] in politics – the conduct of *certain* persons has disgusted me so much that I have a poor opinion of our human nature." LaFontaine was thirty-eight, Baldwin forty-one.

For the outside world they were the self-confident leaders of the movement. They were careful in public to show not even the shadow of a hint of differences between them. Their public demeanour was meant to demonstrate to the citizenry that the election lost in 1844 was a false victory for the old way. They had to remind the public – continuously – that Metcalfe governed with a mediocre cabinet and without Parliament.

The only meaningful breakthrough came immediately after the election. The Reformers were ready to introduce a motion in December 1844 re-establishing French as an official language. In effect, Parliament would pretend it could change the constitution. Draper's government attempted to steal their thunder by doing it themselves, and the law was unanimously passed. Metcalfe and London simply refused to sign the bill. By refusing, they revealed how little they mattered. The representatives of the people of Canada had decided in favour of official bilingualism and proceeded as if that were the case. It was as if London didn't exist.

Meanwhile, politics were far from cleansed of violence. The Reformers won a by-election in Montreal in April 1844. But their victory involved Hincks creating a large gang of armed Irish-Canadian Catholic working-class brawlers from the district of Griffentown. Orange violence met Reform violence, and the Reformers won. It was another case of Hincks's tactical intelligence being detached from ethics. Perhaps this incident laid the foundations for the violence of 1849.

Two months later Baldwin was at a country rally and was chased by "a mob of Orangemen armed with clubs for a considerable distance and I have no doubt would have been severely beaten to say the least of it had we been overtaken."

It's curious that Baldwin, always described as prematurely old, pallid, heavy, was able to outrun a gang of tough thugs. And there he is crossing rough country to public meeting after public meeting, public dinner after public dinner, leading his forces of Upper Canadians toasting and cheering LaFontaine, Lower Canadian Reformers and the voters of Rimouski. And there was LaFontaine constantly on the road, leading Lower Canadian Reformers as they toasted and cheered for Baldwin, Upper Canadian Reformers and the voters of North York. Baldwin went down to Rimouski, where he was carried in triumph out of the ship and through the streets.

Everywhere his message was an incubating one of independence. The words were not quite there, but they were coming. And he had to be careful not to lose the support of those who, although Canadian patriots, still thought fondly of Britain. Baldwin was developing a new vocabulary. Some of it harkened back to 1813, when he had seen the British regulars abandon York. His grandfather and father had been colonels in the militia, he a lieutenant colonel. Now he was saying, "There can be little doubt that the militia will perform their duty if called upon. They have never been backward in defending their country from a foreign force. We want no foreign bayonets here...." Already apparent here is the mindset of the man who in April 1849, with LaFontaine, will prevent the British regulars – foreign bayonets – from firing on the mob, which is what they were trained to do. "I am proud of the connection of Canada with that mighty Empire; I love the Mother Country, but I love the soil on which I live better."

The vote counting of November 1844 was no sooner over than the voters began to treat Metcalfe's victory as an anachronism. Draper had failed, in spite of all his years in power, to build a following among the people. He remained the consummate backroom manoeuvrer, constantly attempting to carve off one Reformer or another. To the extent that he succeeded, their individual reputations were undermined. His was not strengthened.

But once again it was fate that played the cards. Metcalfe had arrived already suffering from cancer. As 1845 ground on, the cancer returned in force, attacking his jaw. By autumn he was blind and incapacitated.

LaFontaine was in Montreal and heard the news first, that the Governor General has sailed off to England. On December 2, himself confined to bed with inflammatory rheumatism, he wrote to Baldwin in triumph. "Lord Metcalfe is gone! Let his friends praise him as much as they please – But as to myself, I will always look upon him as a man who had no respect for the truth, not to use a harsher word."

This comment may seem hard and unforgiving about a man fleeing toward his own death. But LaFontaine and Baldwin had by now seen the imperial and Compact cause repeatedly deliver death as an essential part of their loyalty. Now the Reformers were on the edge of winning power from the citizenry on their own terms. Those of ideas and restraint. This was not a time for romantic hypocrisy. The real world in which they lived was not that of a delusional dying viceroy who for months had not brought himself to leave for home out of fear that Canada would collapse into disorder without him.

Their real world was the politics they had lived with for their entire lives. And so it was intensely linked to place, to family, community and friendship.

Even when caught up in the most difficult of moments, Baldwin would send off a few pages to his four children at school in Quebec City. Some of this concern was guilt, some of it the nineteenth-century father's attempt to exercise authority even at a distance. There was an exchange in December 1845 with his youngest son, Robert, whose birth had brought Eliza's death. The boy was lonely and far from home at Christmas. Yet on the twenty-first his father couldn't resist a correction. "Your letter has 23 lines. This makes the average of your bad spelling only one mistake in eleven lines and a half, which is a great deal better than any of your former letters." Then he catches himself and begins writing to a real child, his own. "We have had a famous skating season this year and I have often wished you and Willey were among the skaters opposite my window to enjoy it."

There he was, staring out from his big house on Front Street across the frozen bay at children skating, while his own, as part of his belief in a new kind of Canada, were eight hundred kilometres away.

CHAPTER SEVEN

Democracy

The last step, the great historic step, would be the easiest. London had been worn down by almost a half-century of political demands from the Canadas and Nova Scotia. The Governors General had failed, one after the other. Their loyal servants, men like Draper, had failed in every attempt to build a conservative following among the voters, in large part because it was colonial conservatism. And the compacts had become dependent on the Orangemen, who were useful for election riots and a handful of seats, but little more.

Yet there was still fear of real change among many middle-class voters. Colonial life brings a certain comfort. You are free to complain about the power that lies far away, while never being yourself fully responsible for your actions. Your risks are limited. Initiatives are left to others. It is a pleasant life. Today we would call it a branch-plant mentality.

It was death that yet again tipped the balance in favour of the democrats. From the early 1840s until 1851 Ireland was in crisis. Its agriculture was a virtual monoculture of pota-toes, which became infected and rotted in the ground. The tenant farmers began to starve. Their absentee landlords, mainly living in London, refused to help. They encouraged emigration. There were 1.5 million or more First Nations and Métis spread across what is now Canada. In the territo-ry of Lower and Upper Canada there were 1.5 million people of European and other origins. The destitute began arriving in that smaller territory. In 1844, 22,000. In 1845, 32,000, then 43,500. The colonies had no control whatso-ever over who, when, how many came.

Then, in 1847, the numbers virtually tripled to 110,000. Most Canadians wanted immigrants. And they wanted experienced farmers, which the Irish were. The problem lay with Ireland's absentee landlords who, like Lord Palmerston, the British foreign minister, were engaged in *human dumping*. They jammed the emigrants on ships in conditions similar to the slave trade – virtually no medical care, no sanitary systems and almost no food. Typhus was soon rampant on the ships, the living and the dead lying together in their excrement. In Montreal Wolfred Nelson witnessed "[o]ld persons, cripples and incurables [sent] to get rid of the expense of providing for them. [W]ithout clothing – without the common necessities of life – [down in the holds] without the air of heaven…. The persons who could be so base, so desperately wicked as to send these poor people here … not caring whether they died on shipboard or on our shores, were guilty of an act worse than murder."

From June to September 1847 Canada took in a 7 percent population increase. Most were quickly sent on from Quebec and Montreal to Upper Canada, where they represented a 15 percent increase. Toronto, with a population of 22,000, took in almost 40,000, moving them on as fast as they could to potential farmland.

About 20 percent of the Irish died. The Canadian government was almost bankrupted by the need to build hospitals, feed the starving, clothe them, send them on their way.

Blame fell in two places: first, on the government in London, and therefore on the Crown; second, on the Canadian government. After all, there was a telegraph system. The mail worked. The government could have known exactly how many ships carrying how many people were on their way. They did not act with due diligence.

The Irish sent on from Montreal to Toronto travelled on ships belonging to a company given a profitable monopoly for immigrant traffic. The conditions on board and on the many barges towed behind were as bad as on the transatlantic slave ships, or worse. This was Family Compact profiteering at its criminal worst.

When the election came in January 1848, hardly a word needed to be said. The government had failed. And they could not, as in the past, invoke loyalty to the old order. The Queen, the Crown and Britain had betrayed Canada and the Irish in a most personal way.

Lord Grey, the British minister of colonies, protested his government's innocence in long, detailed letters to the Governor General. The landlords ordered their estate managers in Ireland to write testimonials of the care they had taken in shipping out their tenants. These were attached to a lengthy report prepared for Grey. It all read like macabre comedy. Lord Palmerston's manager: "[The emigrants] were provided with an abundance of wholesome food and plenty of water.... The greatest attention was paid to them personally by our local Assistants.... The quality of clothing distributed among them just before the vessel sailed surprised everyone, and the people themselves were most thankful."

Lord Grey's justification for non-intervention by the British government was tied, he said, to free trade and market forces; they could neither encourage nor discourage emigration, nor even help the starving without destabilizing the market's natural flow. This rationale was unacceptable nonsense.

The Canadian government began to take control of which and how many people would come in the future and under what conditions. In less than a year we went from being subjected to an emigration policy set in London to an indigenous immigration policy created by an all-party group.

There was one other factor that brought the end of the old political system. In 1843 the Canadian Corn Act had been made law in London, giving Canadian grain a highly preferential tariff. Canada then lowered its tariff on U.S. grain, funnelled that into Canada at a low price and re-exported it on to Britain at a high price. This missing link was a highly profitable present to the Compact businessmen in return for their loyalty in 1837 and during the economic collapse that followed.

Three years later the great English Free Trade movement won its long battle. Britain's Corn Laws were repealed, including the Canadian boondoggle. Britain prospered. Canada fell back into depression. Colonial classes require love from the imperial centre. Now they felt unloved in that most patriotic of places – their pocketbooks.

A new, young Governor General arrived. James Bruce, the Earl of Elgin, was Scottish, and though ambitious for his family and personally without a fortune, he did not carry the English sort of snobbery. He was bilingual and relaxed in public. Lord Grey, the minister Elgin reported to, was his wife's uncle.

Elgin arrived almost certain that he would have to let Responsible Government run its course. And Grey himself actually understood the principle. This was a first for Canada: a colonial minister who believed in Canadian democracy. Even the British prime minister, Lord John Russell, had at last come around. The 1849 Montreal riots would later bring Elgin and Grey a lot of criticism at home, but Russell backed them up in a series of parliamentary debates.

"[In 1836] Mr. Baldwin came to this country.... My opinion when I met him was that I should very widely disagree with him ... but after a long conversation, and mutual explanations, we came to ... nearly entire agreement with respect to the government of Canada." This was of course a complete lie. But they were all shifting their positions and rewriting history to make it seem as if they had not been defeated by mere colonials. Besides, they still saw democracy from the narrowest of perspectives. "The general rule," Russell continued, "would be that you should send to the different parts of the world, and maintain in your different colonies men of the

British race, and capable of governing themselves." Because other races were not capable of governing themselves?

Elgin arrived in Montreal in January 1847, his carriage being dragged with difficulty through the heavy snow. He found a city of 50,000 people comfortable with life in the capital of Canada, three years after its move from Kingston. A small majority of them were anglophone.

The largest and grandest building in the city – the Marché Sainte-Anne – had been transformed at great expense into the Parliament. Like so many markets of that time, it was a neoclassical palace selling food on the ground floor, with two large ballrooms upstairs. It was one hundred metres long, two impressive storeys high, with large, almost floor-to-ceiling windows running close together down either side on both levels. A palace of light. At either end were broad staircases and a great combined portico and balcony held up by Doric columns.

This Parliament sat in what is now Place d'Youville, a hundred metres from where Montreal was founded. The eastern balcony overlooked a new building constructed for the displaced market. The western balcony overlooked McGill Street, more or less the edge of the city.

Engineers had transformed the ground floor into offices for the clerks, the drafters of laws, the translators and other officials. Upstairs, the ballroom overlooking McGill Street was turned into the legislature; at the other end was the upper House. In between was a large tower section with the members' lounges and the parliamentary library – the most important in Canada, holding twenty-three thousand books and the National Archives.

The legislature had a luxurious, airy look, with the windows dominating both sides, heavy curtains, large stuffed chairs for the members and three galleries for five hundred observers. Down the centre of the vaulted ceiling were four large chandeliers with multiple gaslights and red cloth lampshades.

The Governor General's residence was in the country at Monklands, on the west side of the mountain. It had been a rich man's villa. The government put in a private gas-making system to light the house and, in particular, the enormous crystal chandeliers in the ballrooms they had added on either side.

His office, the cabinet room and the government's headquarters were at the eastern end of the city in the old Château Ramezay. There the prime minister and senior ministers worked, backed up by key civil servants in a four-storey stone building behind. They were a two-minute walk away, on the east side, from the new Bonsecours Market and the fashionable Hôtel Rascas, and a two-minute walk on the west side from Place Jacques-Cartier, the municipal guard-house at the top of the Place, Édouard Fabre's bookstore just beyond.

This was the heart of Montreal. Papineau and James McGill lived a minute away, Wolfred Nelson another minute, where the offices of *La Presse* now stand. The Hôtel Nelson on the Place Jacques-Cartier was a gathering spot. George-Étienne Cartier held his wedding party there after marrying Fabre's daughter in Notre Dame. LaFontaine and Morin witnessed the marriage licence.

Baldwin had at first lived in Hôtel Rascas, but then moved out of town to be close to LaFontaine, who had bought a large three-storey formal stone house in Empire style with a mansard roof. It sat high in an orchard sur-rounded by a stone wall. This was in a new area west of the city, just north of Rue Saint-Antoine and south of what is now Canada Square. Baldwin and William Hume Blake took rooms a few minutes away on Saint-Antoine, near today's Hôtel Bonaventure.

From 1847 on, Baldwin's eldest child, Maria, was often with him. The year before, she had turned eighteen, left school in Quebec City and gone to Washington to spend time with American political friends. She regularly reported to her father on local machinations in a time of heightened U.S. nationalism. At one point in their correspondence Baldwin foolishly made a condescending comment about young women and politics. Maria snapped right back. "[D]o you think I have lived all my life among politicians for nothing. No indeed! Politics are with me as though they were a second nature." Within a year she was effectively his private secretary, particularly for everything that had to do with francophones. She had a political insider's sense of French Canada. Some of her work was correspondence, which was of enormous importance, replaced today by phone calls, emails, faxes, memos, policy papers. There were only two ways to communicate – face to face, by letter or, if a few words would do, by telegram.

Baldwin was so dependent on her that when an American professor asked his permission to woo her, he refused, as if the only love story that mattered was his own. The professor quietly went away. No one told Maria what had happened until her father was dead. It was a selfish act by a father who would quit politics a few years later, leaving his daughter with neither a family life of her own nor a political life. Nevertheless, Maria played a real role in Canada's becoming a democracy and in the creation of a society based on co-operation between francophones and anglophones.

THOSE YEARS FROM 1844 TO 1848 were not easy. Draper almost succeeded in tempting René Carin, Quebec City's most powerful politician, into joining the government and thus creating a bi-cultural, pro-colonial conservative party. This move would have split Lower Canada in half.

The two Reform leaders kept reassuring each other that it would all work out, that their strategy was the right one, that they could hold their party together. They worried about whether Elgin would remain as neutral as he insisted he was. They were right to worry. Elgin was complaining in private to Lord Grey about the "unnatural alliance between Baldwin and French factions." Mind you, he was also complaining about "the oligarchy of business-based Anglo-Scottish Tories," who used the secrecy of the Orange Order to control the hustings platforms.

All the while LaFontaine was in physical decline. "[A]fter 2 months of severe illness from which I am not fully recovered I have just got up from my sick bed for the purpose of writing to you. My health is bad … a terrible shock from this last attack of Inflammatory Rheumatism, which, this time extended to the bowels, and produced an abscess which was opened about 12 days ago, and matter is still coming out.… I have had not less than 3 doctors and therefore, I am surprised that I am still living."

Finally, Elgin called an election for January 1848. History has labelled it the great Responsible Government election. But the failure of the established system to deal with the Irish crisis ran like a silent undercurrent through everything. The collapse of the grain trade had confused the Tory merchant class. And Baldwin's promise of a religion-free university system threatened to split the vote.

"ALL MY EXPECTATIONS ... have been realized," LaFontaine wrote to his friend as the votes came in. Thirty-two of forty-two seats in Lower Canada. And Baldwin finally had his Upper Canada majority – twenty-four of forty-two seats. Fifty-six Reformers in all, MacNab and the Tories a miserable eighteen. It was an enormous victory, bigger than anything they had imagined. The voters' intent could not have been more clear.

Rather than resign, the government decided to meet Parliament, which was a good thing. The two months that followed would amount to a step-by-step public demonstration of parliamentary democracy.

The MPs were convened on February 25. MacNab ran for Speaker. Baldwin nominated Augustin-Norbert Morin, who had always wanted the position. He was elected fifty-four to nineteen. Although technically in opposition, the

Reformers took control, in particular of the final shaping of the immigration law.

Then on March 6 Baldwin rose to reply to the Throne Speech: "We feel it to be our humble duty to submit to Your Excellency, that it is essential to the satisfactory result of our deliberations [that your government] should possess the confidence of this House and of the country – and we respectfully represent to Your Excellency that that confidence is not reposed in the present Advisers of your Excellency."

The House supported him fifty-three to twenty-two.

On the seventh, Elgin informed the House that "I shall take measures without delay for forming a new Executive Council."

Since that day in March 1848 the heart of Canadian democracy had been lodged in the confidence of the House. We are not a fixed-term democracy or a presidential democracy. Voters do not choose prime ministers; they choose representatives. And the voters' muscle is expressed through the right of their representatives to give their confidence to governments and to remove it. If the ability of the representatives to give or remove their confidence is interfered with, we are no longer a democracy.

On March 11 the new government was sworn in. It would be known as the Great Ministry. The two friends had been named the attorneys general of Lower and Upper Canada. Baldwin immediately referred to LaFontaine as the "premier." The term *prime minister* quickly became the established public form. As for the cabinet, no one was satisfied. The Reform majority was too big, their coalition very broad. Yet it was not a bad cabinet. There were a few serious radicals like James Price and Louis Michel Viger; some moderates like Colonel Étienne-Paschal Taché – really a red Tory – and James Leslie; creative businessmen like Francis Hincks and William Merritt of Welland Canal fame. For good measure there was the uncertain Quebec City conservative patriot René-Édouard Caron and the unpredictable Malcolm Cameron. Their most dramatic orator was William Hume Blake, solicitor general.

Power seemed to suit LaFontaine and Baldwin. They stopped complaining about their health. In Théophile Hamel's 1848 painting Baldwin looks surprisingly fit and fashionable, with extravagant cuffs on his jacket, a large white stock scarf, and in his hand a brooch, no doubt his wife's, one of those relics of worship that he carried around.

Parliament sat briefly, a session notable only for the immigration bill. There was also a troubling attack on the new government by Louis-Joseph Papineau. He had come back from Paris a year after his amnesty and slowly taken to rumbling against the Reformers. It is always galling to be the former great leader.

Perhaps there was nothing to be done. Papineau was a mass of philosophical and emotional contradictions – alternatively a political radical, an economic and social conservative, an active and severe seigneur to the end of his life. He saw himself as having sacrificed an international, sophisticated life with his return to provincial Canada. To a European friend: "[T]he intellectual life here is so dead, political life so detestable, that I shall live here in misery." He now called for intransigence against his old allies in Upper Canada. Yet among Patriote leaders a deep and broad disappointment in Papineau had been festering for a decade.

Once Parliament had adjourned, the new government set about writing the bills for what would be the most ambitious program the country had ever seen. On January 18, 1849, MPs were summoned to Parliament, and Elgin laid out this program in a Throne Speech, which he read in English and French. The speech confirmed that the old constitutional exclusion of French was gone.

On January 22 Papineau went at the Reformers again. For LaFontaine this attack was deeply insulting. He had tried since 1838 to avoid such a moment. Now it was being forced on him.

And so on January 23 he rose in the House and delivered an almost perfect speech that was the coup de grâce. It had to be done or Papineau would go on trying to divide the francophone half of the party.

> If we had accepted this system of opposition to the bitter end, demanded by the honourable member, Lord Sydenham would have already accomplished his aim: The French Canadians would have been crushed..... No MPs, no place in government, no power; our exiled friends still in exile, our language still proscribed. He himself would still be in forced exile.
>
> To hear him, he alone is virtuous, he alone is courageous, he alone is devoted to the nation!... But since he claims such virtue, I ask him at least to be fair. Where would the honourable member be today, if I had adopted his system of conflict to the bitter end? He would be in Paris, fraternizing, I suppose, with the red republicans, the white republicans or the black republicans and approving, one after the other, the rapidly changing constitutions of France!
>
> He may make these claims, he whose maxim is

let the nation perish rather than a principle. My maxim is quite different – If I perish, so be it, but let us save our compatriots.

PAPINEAU NEVER RECOVERED from this counter-attack. A few years later he would draw a group of interesting young men down the tempting road of what he presented as European liberalism. It was confused with a strange attempt to also include the ultramontane Church. And so he unintentionally went down a dead end, which had the unintended effect of handing more power to the anti-democratic Church.

It is hard for us to feel now what this argument felt like in 1849. And Papineau's agony was only a tiny part of it. Sir Allan MacNab and the compacts were convinced that their right to loyal membership in the British Empire had somehow been stolen from them. The mainstream churches – Catholic, Anglican, Presbyterian, Methodist – were deeply disturbed by the loss of control that democracy represented for them. They had all noticed that LaFontaine and Baldwin, whatever their private beliefs, almost never mentioned religion in their speeches or documents, except to remove it from the structures of public power. But these issues were together but a sideshow to the main event.

What made the date, March 11, 1848, so extraordinary was that the British Empire was then the greatest force in the world, stronger than the United States has ever been. The British had a military, economic and political capacity to enforce their rules that we can no longer imagine. What's more, they repeatedly did enforce them. And combined with a handful of other empires, they had an interlocking global system that one way or another controlled every continent and was far more organized than anything that exists today. Yet LaFontaine, Baldwin and Howe, carrying their movements with them, had somehow succeeded in talking their way – our way – out of the empire's control system and into a new democratic model.

This breakthrough has to be seen in a second context. In 1847 how many countries had a wide franchise as well as a government responsible to their elected parliaments? And how many of those who made democratic reforms in early 1848 managed to hold on to them?

Belgium did. Britain had responsible government, but a very small franchise. The United States survived in good part on a system of industrialized slavery. They were heading into a civil war, and the Senate, as powerful as the president, was more or less appointed until 1913. France popped in and out of various sorts of democracy, falling back into various sorts of dictatorship, and didn't settle down until the 1870s. Even then another coup-cum-dictatorship and civil war lay ahead. As for the Europe-wide democratic movements of 1848, they lasted only a few months.

What was being attempted in Canada and Nova Scotia in early 1848 was not a matter of colonial catch-up. LaFontaine and Baldwin in particular were leading us almost first out of the modern democracy gate.

How it would work, its effect on society and on the well-being of the people, whether a broad popular franchise was the right basis for a stable government system, whether business would be helped or harmed – all of this was unknown. Did they understand how far out on the cutting edge they were? Probably not, because so many others were trying at the same time. Why the Canadian experiment would last while most of the others would collapse is perhaps a mystery, but it was not an accident.

CHAPTER EIGHT

Loyalty

When serious reformers win major electoral battles, they believe a great threshold has been crossed. Curiously enough, these victories are usually a prelude to the real struggle.

Those who have won need time to restructure the state. The losers, therefore, have a small window of time to find a cause so dramatic that it will wipe out the consensus of the recent election.

The battle that began in Canada on Tuesday, February 13, 1849, and stretched on into the autumn turned on one particularly controversial bill: the Rebellion Losses Bill for Lower Canada. Actually there was nothing controversial about it. A virtually identical bill had been introduced several years before by Draper's Conservative government. It had compensated citizens in Upper Canada who had lost property in the fighting of 1837 and had not themselves been rebels. The bill had passed with little controversy; an independent commission examined the claims; the money was paid out. And that was that.

Draper's government had then prepared an equivalent bill for losses in Lower Canada, using the same rules. Perhaps nervous about the Orangemen when it came to giving money to Catholics, they had not taken the bill further. After all, a lot of the compensation would go to innocent francophone farmers and village people whose houses had been burnt down by a rampant Château Clique militia.

LaFontaine, seconded by Baldwin, introduced a revised version of the old Conservative bill on February 13. He did it in a cool, low-key way.

For the compacts, the Orangemen and the Conservatives, bound together in an awkward coalition under Sir Allan MacNab, this initiative had potential – perhaps enough to wipe out any memory of the voters' recent decision to support democracy and the Reform platform. MacNab was one of those virtually bankrupted by the repeal of the Corn Laws. He needed to be in office to produce an income. But first his party would have to create a crisis of loyalty. Loyalty in populist rhetoric is always about patriotism, as in "patriotism, the last refuge of a scoundrel." In this case loyalty would be about the Crown, Britain, the Anglo-Saxon race.

The trick would be to paint LaFontaine's brand-new government as a coalition of traitors – a ministry of former rebels handing out loyalist money to former rebels – and so force the Governor General to remove it, causing a reversion to the old, loyal, colonial system. They remained convinced that the imperial leaders had not abandoned them. But then they were not reading Elgin's official letters to his masters in London. "Bear in mind that I am presiding over one of the most democratic communities that ever existed – that [Canada's] constitution is most popular in character, elected by a very extensive constituency." Even if they had read this, the Tories would probably have believed they could under-mine democratic sympathies by simply setting anglophones and francophones at each other's throats.

THE MOMENT LAFONTAINE was back in his seat, the Tory front bench began working their strategy. Colonel John Prince jumped to his feet: "The people of Upper Canada would cut off their hands rather than pay these claims" to former rebels. Henry Sherwood, the outgoing Conservative leader: "Such a system would be an open encouragement to rebel-lion, as the parties engaged would be insured that if they failed in their schemes they should be indemnified for their losses."

Both knew this was untrue, but they hoped to sow doubt among all those anglophones, far away in Upper Canada,

reliant on sensationalist newspapers. Two days of this taunting followed.

LaFontaine and Baldwin were too self-controlled and
far too focused to rise to the bait. But Hincks was the third
Reformer up. He foolishly began describing equivalent jus-
tifiable past revolutions against tyrants in England. Then,
carried away, he threw out, "The honourable gentlemen
are indignant against those who took up arms in 1837 and
1838 – but who was responsible for the disturbances if not
the honourable gentlemen opposite? ... Their government
was carried on in such an unconstitutional manner that
the people were perfectly justified in taking up arms to
oppose it."

He had lunged at the bait. The Opposition began arguing that the proposed payments were to be made to rebels
because the government supported rebellion. They were
"dangerous, criminal and subversive of order."

Suddenly Wolfred Nelson was on his feet backing
Hincks. "What? Is it rebellion to insist on your constitutional rights and to resist if they are violated?" MacNab accused
him of defying the law.

Nelson: "There was no law then."

MacNab: "Were you not a rank rebel!"

Nelson: "Not to my God!"

MacNab: "But against your country, against your oath of allegiance, and against the laws of your country."

Drawing on what Hincks had said, MacNab went a step further. If his own party had been responsible for the rebellion, then the government was making them into the rebels. "I have never been called a rebel until tonight.... Do you think the Loyalists of Upper Canada have no feelings? No affection? Are we to be told by our government that we were the rebels?"

MacNab was developing an argument that might spread fear among the Upper Canadians. Hincks and others, suddenly seeing the danger, tried to calm the situation by insisting that they had never called MacNab a rebel, but MacNab simply went on insisting they had, and by extension they were accusing all loyal Upper Canadians of the same thing.

For a dozen years all of this resentment had been festering just under the surface. The Reformers, whether rebels or not, had never got over the damage done by the corruption of the compacts and their indifference to the public good. And the men who saw themselves as the Loyalists, who had put down the 1837 rebellion and resumed governing in the old way, could never understand why they had received so little credit for their service. They, loyal servants of the

Crown, were gradually being reduced to the villains and fools of history.

Hincks and Nelson had lanced the boil, and over the next two weeks all the poison came oozing out. They were struggling over myth. Who would be declared by history to have been on the side of right and justice?

MacNab launched into a particularly long and overwrought defence of the loyal men of the Compact. "[T]he people of Upper Canada will never pay the losses of Lower Canadian rebels." Baldwin's Upper Canadian reformers "were under the dominion of French masters." The constitution of 1840 "was intended to reduce the Lower Canadians to the dominion of the British Canadians and the contrary had been brought about." The government benches mocked him and he shouted at them – "You laugh to see the Anglo-Saxons under your feet." Well, "if they were to be ruled by foreigners," better it should be by Americans than Frenchmen. To call French Canadians foreigners was calculated to define the struggle along racial lines.

LaFontaine and Baldwin could sense that all of this was gradually prying open the Pandora's box of racial politics. Hincks again tried to calm things and draw the debate onto more intellectual ground. But it was too late. By the next day MacNab's people were out across Upper Canada spreading the word that they were to pay for French rebels. The Orange Order and the St. Andrew's Society of Montreal were in their element.

Two days later the House came back to the bill with the galleries jammed. This was clearly the best show in Montreal. Society ladies were at the front, a more dubious mixture of citizens behind them.

The cabinet minister James Price was first up and began to taunt the Tories. "[T]he parties engaged in the rebellion might be blamed, but those who by their misrule had provoked rebellion were more to blame. [Their] arbitrary tyrannical manner turned the government into an oligarchy. [MacNab's] loyalty was only the loyalty of the pocket." He dared the Opposition to call him a rebel.

This was only a warm-up to what would be the great speech of the debate, the one that ensured disorder would follow. William Hume Blake, the solicitor general for Upper Canada, had an extravagant, theatrical style, at first almost comic, but gradually drawing you in with his intelligence and mesmerizing approach.

He began with a meticulous deconstruction of the compacts and their policies before launching into high drama. "They have recklessly seized the torch of discord, which we had hoped had long since been extinguished, and lighted it anew through the length and breadth of our country, regardless though this wanton procedure should involve in anarchy and ruin the whole frame and structure of our social system.... They dare to take this torch of discord, and cast it flaming amongst the inhabitants of the country.... I feel they should move an amendment, and propose the erection of a gibbet before every French Canadian's door, and offer up an holocaust of 700,000 men to appease the British feeling of Canada."

He analyzed their actions over a half-century, slicing MacNab and the Opposition into tiny pieces. "The administration of justice was perverted; the dearest rights of man were violated with impunity; human life was not sacred; and worse still, aye, a thousand times worse, a loyal but contemptible minority seized on every office in the gift of the Crown, and trampled on men far superior to themselves in every sense of the word." Morin tried desperately to keep order as enraged people cried out from the galleries. Blake pressed on.

"True loyalty guards the liberty of the subject, with a care at least equal to that with which it protects the prerogative of the Crown. Their loyalty, ever ready to extend and strengthen the prerogative of the Crown by stinting and limiting the liberties of the people, is not loyalty – it is slavery.

All history teems with examples of this pliant quality falsely called Loyalty by the honourable gentlemen opposite, this spurious Canadian Loyalty.

"And there sit the loyal men" – he stabbed his finger at the Opposition – "who shed the blood of the people and trampled on their best and dearest rights."

Blake, like a great actor of the nineteenth-century school, had lifted the tension in the House to dangerous levels. Then came his final peroration, which was felt like an explosion: "I tell those honourable and loyal gentlemen, so highly offended the other day at having the term *rebel* applied to them, that I call them rebels, and they must not expect any apologies from my mouth."

MacNab instantly leapt to his feet, calling Blake a liar. Fighting broke out in the galleries. MacNab demanded that Blake withdraw his accusation. "Never!" The generalized brawl in the galleries was so bad that the women had to be saved by lifting them onto the floor of the House. Morin sent the sergeant-at-arms and his men to stop the fighting. Then MacNab and Blake threw themselves on each other.

LaFontaine and Baldwin seem to have sat quietly through it all.

The next day, Friday, John A. Macdonald, a young and first-time Kingston MP and still an Orange Order supporter, was prevented from fighting a duel with Blake. The weekend served only to increase the tensions as word spread of the debate and Orange meetings led to fighting in small towns throughout the country.

On Tuesday LaFontaine intervened with a long, careful analysis, intentionally boring, attempting to get back to the procedural approach. He warned the Opposition that he was indifferent to "their insults, their incessant attacks, launched to disgust him or intimidate him!" The government would not be intimidated. But what they would not stand for was the growing attacks on the Governor General, who was only doing his job by staying neutral. LaFontaine allowed himself one emotional response to MacNab's having called French Canadians foreigners. "Il les a appelés foreigners, étrangers! Quoi! Les canadiens-français foreigners on their native land!"

That night government MPs began to complain that it was improper for Opposition MPs to be egging on "unruly and riotous mobs in this city," as had been the method of the Jacobins in the French Revolution. That was how the autocratic forces in Europe had encouraged disorder in the summer of 1848, which led to the overthrowing of one democratic government after another.

The debate turned into a histrionic filibuster as the Tories dragged it out, using the time to build anger and confusion throughout Upper Canada. It went on twenty-four hours a day; members stretched out or slumped on the Speaker's steps and the gallery benches. The Tories just kept on repeating that loyal Anglo-Saxons would have to pay rebel French Canadians. And the government kept denying that was so. The bill was perfectly clear, but this whole debate was about myth, not law. Late on the twenty-seventh Baldwin spoke, laying out the facts to no effect. This was not his kind of argument. In March the painful voting process began, with endless amendments intended to produce more delay.

On March 2 the Opposition began openly threatening Elgin. They had petitions. The people were angry. Colonel Prince: "This is a voice Lord Elgin must listen to." Colonel Gugy: "I hope the Governor General will have enough courage ... his personal honour is committed to the maintenance of the integrity of the Empire.... The Governor General should act as a mediator amid conflicting parties.... Who is the guardian in this Colony? Not the majority in this House surely. No, but the Governor General alone." In other words, they believed their strategy had worked: that they had created a disorder in the land negating the clear election results of fourteen months before and therefore requiring the arbitrary intervention of the Governor General over and against the confidence of the House. It was a matter of loyalty to the Crown.

Elgin wrote home to his minister, Lord Grey: "The Tory party are doing what they can by menace, intimidation and appeals of passion to drive me to a coup d'état." Finally, on March 9, the bill went through.

FOR THE NEXT SIX WEEKS calm appeared to return to the legislature. The Reform agenda progressed. Laws were passed. But the tension was there under the surface and the Tory Loyalty campaign, now in full swing in the constituencies, was focused on Elgin. He was warned again and again that he must not sign the bill. Unsigned it was meaningless, and so was Responsible Government.

That spring the ice went out early and ships began arriving at Quebec City. But nothing could be landed until the new customs bill, with important revenue implications, had been signed. It was an urgent financial matter. Elgin had been staying out of town to avoid being drawn into the Rebellion Losses Bill controversy, so there were forty-two bills waiting to be signed into law.

At 4 p.m. on Wednesday, April 25, he arrived in a coach with a few liveried servants and a light escort at the east end of Parliament abutting the market. He was escorted upstairs to the Legislative Council, where he signed all forty-two in rapid succession, without comment, including that on Rebellion Losses, got up and was escorted out, pausing on the way to chat with some officials. The word was spreading. Even LaFontaine and Baldwin, who knew full well that this was how Responsible Government worked, were caught off guard.

By the time he got downstairs there was a large crowd outside. The market stalls were only a few metres away, and hands were filled with eggs and vegetables. As Elgin came out from under the great porch they began booing. His aide de camp whispered, "They're just low-life, Excellency."

"Well-dressed low-life," Elgin muttered. As he walked to his carriage the eggs and tomatoes began flying. He was soaked by the time the horses pulled away at great speed.

The Montreal *Gazette* rushed out a special evening edition, and their newsboys scattered into the streets – "THE DISGRACE OF GREAT BRITAIN ACCOMPLISHED." "CANADA SOLD AND GIVEN AWAY!" Elgin signing the law was "to the eternal and damnable disgrace of Great Britain." "Rebellion is the Law of the Land!" Elgin would be "the last Governor of Canada."

As night fell, the fire brigade – a Protestant-controlled force – rushed a truck through the streets ringing its bell and calling loyal Britons to a mass meeting on the Champs-de-Mars, just across the gardens on the north side of the Château Ramezay. At 8 p.m. Colonel Gugy, a front-bench Tory MP, began haranguing the crowd of five thousand, turning them into a mob, with the standard help of strong drink and the dramatic light and darkness produced by the sea of hand-held torches. At about 9 p.m. the captain of the hook, ladder and hose brigade, Alfred Perry, climbed up on the platform to read a petition to the Queen. Instead, he extinguished his torch, shouting, "The time for petitions has passed. If you are in earnest, follow me to Parliament House!" And the mob set off up to Rue Notre-Dame, spilling through the city, yelling, breaking the windows of houses and businesses belonging to Reformers, down to Rue Saint-François-Xavier, St. Peter Street, to McGill Street and the Legislative Assembly. Twenty minutes through the streets with their voices echoing off the facades gave them extra courage.

A lot has been written about Alfred Perry. And he did a lot of boasting through his long life about what happened that night. The impression created is of what the English call a soccer lout. Full of himself, racist, fast to violence and happy to be attacking someone of another race or religion.

The legislature was sitting late, half empty, Morin in the Speaker's Chair, Blake and MacNab across from each other,

Sandfield Macdonald, the future premier of Ontario, and others in their places. As the mob spilled around the building, the parliamentary ushers locked the doors from the inside. Perry organized the long, heavy fire truck ladder as a battering ram, and on the second charge the doors under the great porch were broken in. A dozen of the rioters charged up the stairs and into the legislature, knocking down the sergeant-at-arms, beating Sandfield Macdonald unconscious. The MPs fought back, including the Tories, for whom things had suddenly gone too far. MacNab, aging and overweight, was nevertheless a born brawler and found himself unexpectedly on the same side as Blake. Morin refused to leave the authority of his Chair. Heavy glass ink pots flew. The parliamentarians fought with anything they could lay their hands on and gradually drove Perry and his men out of the chamber and back down to the street.

There Perry gathered some extra men from the mob and charged up again. This time they overwhelmed the MPs, who withdrew into the centre of the building. One rioter seized the mace, another sat in the Speaker's Chair shouting crude remarks. Paving stones began raining through the windows from the thousands of men below, striking anyone in the chamber. One hit a gaslight, setting its shade on fire. Soon the whole legislature was in flames. Some MPs tried to save books from the library, others the paintings. Eventually they had to save themselves. The firemen were unavailable. They were otherwise occupied.

By 2 a.m. the Parliament of Canada was a smouldering shell. Twenty-three thousand books had been lost, all of our archives, historic portraits, all three a treasure trove stretching back to New France. None of this seemed to bother the Orangemen or merchants from the St. Andrew's Society. But the theme of lost books and lost archives would be endlessly lamented in speech after speech over the weeks to come, both by those defending the government and those attacking it. With this destruction of knowledge Canada had demeaned itself.

The next morning at nine the House assembled upstairs at the far end of the vast West Ballroom of the unfinished Bonsecours Market, unheated and unfurnished. It looks today as it did then, except the vaulted ceiling was still bare timbers. The Speaker sat on a rough market bench. There were a few more benches for the older MPs. The others stood in the cold.

MacNab wanted a debate about the riot and the government's failure to protect Parliament. But the prime minister simply didn't appear. He was where he had been all night, around the corner in the Château Ramezay, attempting to manage the continuing disorder. Baldwin took the floor, his habit of inaudible mumbling even more pronounced in the cavernous hall. He moved the creation of a committee to reconstitute the written legislative program of the House, which would include redrafting the bills. Everything had been lost in the fire, and the government's response was that they would neither be diverted from their program nor delayed. In other words, a legislature is not a room. It is the elected representatives of the people and a legislative program. Let the rioters riot. The government would get on with reforming the country. The Tories could not believe what they were hearing. They had wanted a crisis, even if things had got rather out of hand. Now the Reformers were acting as if nothing had happened. It was the difference between people who believed that power was order and property versus people who believed that power was the application of ideas and ethics.

Meanwhile the mob was reconstituting itself, taking over the downtown, surrounding both the Bonsecours Market and the Château Ramezay. LaFontaine ordered out what little professional army there was in town to protect both. Later in the day he briefly went outside the protective ring and had to be saved from the mob by a few soldiers.

His orders were clear: maintain order but do not open fire. Baldwin was in full agreement. Elgin made it clear that he would put up with any personal humiliation "but if I can possibly prevent it, no stain of blood shall rest upon my name." General d'Urban, the senior officer in Canada, had been in Sorel and rushed back to Montreal. He was given strict orders not to use overt force. D'Urban was an old, experienced soldier, but no one had ever ordered him to control a mob without using force. Restraint, restraint, restraint. The chief rioters were arrested, but there were only sixty policemen in Montreal. So when the mob gathered to storm the jail, Perry and his friends were released. A police militia of Irish Catholics and French Canadians was created under the command of a cabinet minister, Colonel Taché. As soon as d'Urban had brought enough professional soldiers into town, the militia was disbanded.

But the mob still controlled the streets, and that evening, Thursday, April 26, they set off to attack the houses of the Reformers – Nelson's house near the Champs-de-Mars, Hincks's house up on Beaver Hill – then they marched west along Saint-Antoine, damaging the house in which Baldwin and Blake were staying, and kept on to LaFontaine's new house. There they broke down the gates, burned down the stables, then invaded his home, burning the furniture, smashing everything, throwing his large library out into a pile and putting it to flames. Neither the prime minister nor

Adèle was there. They had discreetly taken refuge in a hotel near the Château Ramezay. Months later the hotel owner sent LaFontaine an outrageously inflated bill.

In spite of this generalized violence and disorder, the cabinet held a historic meeting the next day, Friday, April 27. They all agreed to a strategy laid out in a report by William Merritt, which formalized their philosophy of restraint. "[T]he proper mode of preserving order is by strengthening the civil authorities…. The Committee of Council deprecates the employment of the military to suppress such disturbances as those which have disgraced the City of Montreal." This strategy was unprecedented in Western societies.

Tories, Conservatives and supporters of the rioters have always insisted that it wasn't a strategy, it was weakness; that LaFontaine and Baldwin were afraid to give orders that would not be obeyed. Francophone nationalists have always been in a strange sort of agreement with their enemies: the *Anglo-Saxons* were unwilling to shoot their own.

Both sides miss the point. General d'Urban had several thousand British regulars who would obey orders. When it came to British soldiers in the British Empire, the rules were perfectly simple. To disobey orders would lead to their own execution. What's more, it was 1849. Western armies had been shooting down their own race, their own class, their own family everywhere; 1848–49 in the West was all about a prolonged civil war within the bourgeoisie. And if LaFontaine and Baldwin insisted on restraint it was because they believed it to be the only way. Elgin risked his career by agreeing with them. Lord Grey had always backed him up, but not on this – not on restraint. Grey to Elgin, June 1: "[W]hen the question of firing on the mob arises it is far better on every ground to trust to the regular Troops.... Napoleon was right ... the most merciful way of using Troops in civil commotions was not to fire until the last extremity but when the necessity came to fire in earnest and if possible not throw away a shot." That point of *last extremity* had been passed on the evening of April 25. The belief of the three leaders in Montreal was simple: if the cost of avoiding a bloodbath and a permanent division based on race was some riots and a few burnt buildings, so be it.

On Saturday the twenty-eighth, the House voted its "Address of thanks to Lord Elgin." As described in Chapter 1, the Governor General came to town on Monday afternoon to receive this address and was lucky to escape with his life.

All was not negative. Loyal democrats were streaming out to Monklands to reassure Elgin, the first group led by George-Étienne Cartier. A shipload of Reformers came up

from Quebec City to do the same. An angry mob was waiting for them at the downtown wharfs, but they were warned
and so docked upstream and went on by coach.

On May 10 a ship carrying a delegation of twenty-five
Toronto Reform leaders from Toronto, Kingston and
Cobourg arrived unexpectedly and went straight out to pay
their respects to Elgin. That night at seven-thirty the cabinet
entertained them with dinner on the ground floor of the
Hôtel Têtu on Rue Saint-James.

Word spread and the mob began to gather outside,
throwing paving stones through the windows, then broke
down the doors and rushed in. Blake pulled out his pistol.
In the fighting that followed he wounded two, perhaps a
first and last for a solicitor general. Then the troops arrived
and cleared the street.

All through the spring and summer, letters poured in to
Baldwin from alarmed Reform leaders around Upper
Canada, warning of possible uprisings. The Second
Battalion of the Lenox Militia apparently had a commanding officer and senior officers who "are men of violent tem-
pers and conduct." They had access to the regiment's arms,
"which might very readily be had access to by the
Orangemen." The arms, therefore, had to be seized. There
were dozens of such weapon stocks accessible to Compact

men, Tories and Orangemen because they controlled so much of the militia.

But LaFontaine and Baldwin stuck to their strategy. Everything was done to calm people's nerves. Elgin stayed out at Monklands, where his wife had given birth to their first child on May 16. The two friends stayed downtown, running the government. At the end of May, Parliament rose for the summer, and the MPs returned to their constituencies with their tales of justice or injustice. The economy continued to collapse, and Montreal merchants felt it most. With Parliament in recess, the city's newspapers lost interest in the Rebellion Losses Law and instead began calling for annexation by the United States.

On July 26 the Tories held a convention in Kingston and voted in favour of annexation. If they could not control Canada, and if London was not going to offer economic advantages, they would take their business elsewhere.

Early on August 15 six men involved in the burning of Parliament were arrested. A large mob gathered in protest and took over the downtown, barricading the streets. The army managed to disperse them, but they reassembled in the evening and began slowly marching down Rue Saint-Antoine heading once again for LaFontaine's house two and a half kilometres away. As there had been rumours all day of a plot to assassinate him, LaFontaine sent for troops. None appeared. His cabinet minister Colonel Taché quickly pulled together eleven friends with militia experience. They barricaded the house and armed themselves with rifles at the windows up on the first floor. Adèle was there. LaFontaine was with Taché, watching out the windows.

Around 10 p.m. the mob appeared and broke down the metal gates, surging toward the house, throwing paving stones. Firing broke out on both sides. The stone facade was pockmarked with bullet holes. In the other direction six men were wounded, and a young man called William Mason died of his wounds. It was 10:30 p.m. before the soldiers arrived and cleared the mob away.

Three days later, fifteen hundred people followed Mason's body through the streets, the hearse hung with crimson drapery, the young men with blood-red bandanas around their heads. On the twentieth LaFontaine was summoned to testify before the coroner's inquiry into Mason's death. It was held upstairs in the Hôtel Cyrus on Place Jacques-Cartier. He was a few minutes into his testimony when smoke began billowing up from below. The hotel had been set on fire in an attempt to kill him. The prime minister, coroner and twelve jurors rushed downstairs through the smoke before they became trapped and then out onto the square, where the mob was waiting. In a protective bubble created by soldiers of the Seventy-first Highlanders, with bayonets fixed, they were moved for safety to the top of the square into the Municipal Guard House. The painter Napoléon Bourassa happened to witness the scene and commented that LaFontaine walked through the screaming mob calmly, as if they were not there. "Imperturbable."

In the guardhouse LaFontaine insisted that they continue the inquiry. When you read his cool, even serene, testimony, it has a surreal air about it. The prime minister of Canada, barricaded with his wife in his house, protected by a cabinet minister and a few friends with rifles, a riot, a gun battle. And there he was a few days later describing it all in his lawyerly manner in a guardhouse with two hundred Scottish soldiers, bayonets fixed, holding off the mob outside.

This atmosphere of crisis and disorder had now lasted seven months, and there were still two dramas to come. In mid-September, 325 leading Tories and francophone nationalists – in other words, enemies of each other – came together to sign the Annexation Manifesto. The francophones represented a new generation of nationalists, and Papineau made it clear that he agreed with them. As Eric Bédard puts it, they saw annexation as rational, republican, clearly anti-colonial, "a sort of act of faith in the future."

The annexation movement had many causes. The economic collapse. The shift of power to a mixed-religion group of democrats. The feeling among extreme nationalist francophones was that they were the real victims, and the past was a prison. The desire of the Tories and these French-Canadian nationalists not to have a real relationship, and therefore to replace the British Empire with a new arbitrator – the United States.

It was a classic colonial expression of insecurity. In fact, both parties would have been destroyed by integration into the United States – the pampered compacts crushed in the open market, French and its culture sucked into oblivion. Neither seemed to pay attention to the fate of Hispanics on the southern United States border, or the slave-dependent half of the U.S. economy, or the unprecedented levels of corruption by any Western standards in the United States Congress. What was it that united this improbable group – young, French-Canadian nationalists, liberal in the pure nineteenth-century English tradition, like Antoine-Aimé Dorion, with old-fashioned Compact Tories like the Molsons, McGills and Redpaths? Dorion, a future Canadian Liberal Party leader, was one of two official secretaries of the Annexation Association.

What these people shared was an inability to deal with

the new Canadian politics – politics in which the clarity of money and race and ideology, so common and modern in Europe and the United States, were being melted into something much more complicated and deeply un-European; something complicated enough to allow Canadians to live together. They were disturbed by this confusing new model of statehood, which struck them as unclear and immoral precisely because it lacked rational clarity. It was the same desire for rational clarity in the construction of nation-states that would produce one hundred million deaths in the century-long civil war that followed in Europe.

LaFontaine and Baldwin agreed that Elgin should give those who signed the Annexation Manifesto a clear choice: recant, or be removed from any possible link to public office, and therefore the public purse. The government then set about working on the economy, and in particular on trade with the United States. Most of the annexationists fell into line. In effect, the battle over who would define loyalty had been decided. The compacts had thrown away all self-respect by abandoning the Crown in favour of the republic they had always claimed to detest.

The final drama stretched out over August and September. Lord and Lady Elgin had stayed out of Montreal since April. Now they set off from Monklands on a series of official tours through Upper Canada. It was, after all, Upper Canada that MacNab's party been trying to win back with their anti-democratic, anti–French Canadian crisis. Elgin threw himself and his wife into the hands of this Protestant citizenry for safekeeping. They travelled almost alone, without soldiers or police, with a retinue of two. The citizenry would have to take responsibility for them. The risk was calculated, but it was a real risk.

In between two of these tours, Elgin wrote a moving letter to Baldwin that expresses just how close to the wind they were all sailing. He began calmly enough, with careful handwriting and ordered thoughts, but gradually slipped into an agitated script as he gave instructions for what ought to be done if he were assassinated.

> I start from here on Monday with the intention of visiting in the same manner.... I hope to be able to conciliate parties so far at least as to prevent collision [in spite of] the deeply gangrened condition of the public mind. Should my journey have a different issue from that I expect and the fanaticism of individuals or factions hurry them on to the commission of a great crime, it will be for the Government to consider whether Parliament

> should not at once be called and measures taken to ensure the supremacy of law and order.... This memo may be of use in the communication of the Govt. With General Rowan.

Behind the scenes, dozens of letters were flying back and forth between Baldwin and every trustworthy Reformer he could mobilize throughout the province as he micromanaged Elgin's trip. Elgin, so eager to keep out of politics, was now on the ultimate Responsible Government tour.

As he moved about, local leaders had to choose where they stood. Some left town to avoid choosing. If a town were too dangerous, Elgin was escorted around it. The makeup of every welcoming party, the shape of every appearance, who would speak, who would be allowed on the platform, the words on every welcome arch and on every banner were all negotiated in detail. If one town went well, a nearby town might agree to receive him the next day. Or not. In which case a way around had to be found in a province with very few passable roads. These plans didn't always work. In London, for example, groups of thugs rushed about firing shots and knocking down triumphal arches. At the municipal welcome, the mayor was scarcely civil. In other towns the reception was rapturous.

Gradually local Tories began to co-operate. They wanted to be on the official platform in their own town, provided that they could make a speech attacking the Reform government, in return for which they would express their support for the Governor General. In other words, they were publicly accepting Responsible Government and real democracy.

ALL OF THIS LOOKS EASY after the fact, just as Responsible Government and democracy now seem to have been inevitable. But in most Western countries there was nothing inevitable about either until a century later, usually after 1945 or 1962 or 1989.

The miracle of 1849 was that LaFontaine and Baldwin, with the full co-operation of Elgin, invented a new form of politics that would later be picked up by men like Gandhi and Mandela. They did this by refusing conflict, no matter how unbearable the taunts. In all, a dozen or so people died, not the tens of hundreds or thousands expected or the hundreds of thousands experienced in most other countries. The possibility of another idea of loyalty was affirmed – loyalty to the public good.

Often in the telling of our history these months of disorder are rushed over in embarrassment. If mentioned, these unpleasant moments are dealt with as accidents, isolated events, not of great importance. If you go to the places where all of this took place, there are no signs, no plaques, no statues.

It is as if the grand Parliament of Sainte-Anne's, where we became a democracy, had never existed, as if our first prime minister had not governed from the Château Ramezay. Even LaFontaine's house, of enormous historical importance, barely survives in the midst of property-development battles.

But if we do not understand the persistent intensity of violence in 1849 and the persistent restraint of LaFontaine and Baldwin in response, we cannot understand what Canada would have become had they weakened at any moment.

CHAPTER NINE

The Use of Power

The two friends had survived these months of violence unruffled, unperturbed, at least on the surface. But survival was not their purpose. During their first real parliamentary session, from January 18 to May 30, 1849, the period of greatest disorder, they had worked almost two hundred laws through the House.

A few days before Parliament was burnt down, Baldwin, in one of his greatest triumphs, introduced the act creating the University of Toronto. He wrenched higher education out of the hands of the churches with their English class model, and created a new model for Canadian public universities. It was completely secular. The usual suspects called it "entirely infidel." Even though later governments would loosen his rules, Baldwin's model was used to create the English-language university system across the country. During the Quiet Revolution it influenced the reform of Quebec's universities. And it remains in place to this day.

The University Bill vote took place on Montreal's last real day as the capital of Canada. The violence of its Scottish merchants and their Orange supporters had lost the city its right to lead. The capital was moved in the autumn of 1849 on a rotating basis to Toronto then Quebec City. The first parliamentary session in Toronto was just as productive as that in Montreal.

During 1849 and 1850 LaFontaine, Baldwin and Hincks divided their initiatives into three parcels. Hincks used long-term strategies to revive the economy: the big commercial waterway projects, the St. Lawrence and Welland canals, were completed. He developed a new approach to building railways, particularly long-distance railways, including what would become the interprovincial link from Quebec City to Halifax. He established government subsidies for building railway systems, an approach that would lead eventually to the cross-country Canadian Pacific Railway. The Reformers believed that open communications, including the easy movement of citizens, were central to building a democratic society, as well as to wealth creation.

In the middle of the political crisis Hincks was sent off to London, where he accomplished a miracle by educating and calming the majority of imperial leaders who were convinced that rebels had taken power in the colonies.

Meanwhile, LaFontaine and Baldwin had begun working dozens of bills through Parliament aimed at creating a modern legal system, one that was open and accessible. They created divisional courts, decentralizing justice so that poorer people could get at it. They created the modern Canadian jury system. They created an appeals court, a Just Assessment system, a notarial system, a title-registration system, cleaned up corporate law, increased the independence of judges by banning them from all other functions. They abolished imprisonment for debt. "[I]mprisonment is inconsistent with that forbearance and humane regard to the misfortunes of others which should always characterize legislation...." They put supports in place for poor people who wanted to sue. "[I]t is unjust to refuse access to the Courts to suitors whose pecuniary means are insufficient to enable them to pay." They put Wolfred Nelson in charge of cleaning up the corrupt and violent prison system.

Baldwin led the way in removing "the Right of Primogeniture in the Succession of Real Estate." This old English system, handing all family property to the eldest male, was and remains central to the British class system. With this law Baldwin destroyed both his own father's dream of a Whig aristocracy in Canada and his own eldest son's prospects.

The government took over the post office, turning it into a system for egalitarian communications. How? By standardizing and lowering the postal rates, while opening post offices in as many communities as possible. They put through a comprehensive public school act for Upper Canada, created separate schools for Upper Canadian Catholics, further reformed the Election Act, got London to repeal its Navigation Act with its limitations on who had access to British ports. Now the ports were Canadian, and in the next season more than one hundred non-British vessels appeared.

The single most powerful piece of democratic progress was the Municipal Corporations Act, often called the Baldwin Act. It extended the principles of parliamentary democracy to the cities, towns and villages and removed at least overt power from the landowners.

These are only a few samples of the legal and social initiatives undertaken in fewer than three years that produced the foundations of modern Canada. The reality of an apolitical, professional civil service was seriously advanced. The first pieces of a union system designed to protect workers and improve work conditions were put in place.

When we look back it all appears simple. The dramas of violence catch our attention, with good reason. The

Reformers held on in Canada while they failed elsewhere. But such physical dramas cause us to overlook what could be called a revolution in assumptions. These new assumptions about the nature of the public good changed the country's direction. Without anyone consciously understanding the links, the country was realigning itself on a non-linear, non-British, non-European approach that stretched back into Aboriginal civilizations. With the waterfall of legislation put through by the Great Ministry, LaFontaine and Baldwin had yanked Canada out of its colonial mimicry and set it off in an interesting direction.

THERE WERE ALSO SERIOUS FAILURES. The Clergy Reserve tangle would have to be solved by others. Divisions among Lower Canadian Reformers left the seigneurial system in place for a few more years.

The most disappointing failure came over votes for women. Under the old electoral system, the franchise was tied to property ownership. If a woman happened to own property, she could vote. And they did. In the 1830s female suffrage was at first more common in Lower Canada, then the Upper Canadian women caught up. This right was removed in 1850, and with that Canada fell into line with other Western democracies.

Why did a Reform government remove this right? Part of the answer involves the decline of rural, more co-operative societies and the rise of the industrial state in which the male was reduced to a factory and office slave. He rediscovered his self-respect by advancing the idea of the fragile sex, which required the self-deification of the male – the great protector.

There was also a local particularity. Women voters tended to be richer, and thus Tory. The drunken club-wielding gangs around the hustings platforms often meant that to vote you had to fight your way to the platform. Only a rich woman could afford the armed gang necessary to provide a protective circle. In the 1840s a notable number of ridings were won at the last moment by the Compact thanks to the late appearance of well-protected groups of women voters. And so landowning women came to be seen by the Reformers as part of the corruption of the old system.

There is one other related factor. It is evident in letters and articles of the time that politics was a filthy, corrupt, drunken, violent business – men at their worst. Thank God for the purity of women, who through the family could save the men. For the sake of the power produced by their purity, women had to be protected from the impure brutality of politics. Thus nineteenth-century romanticism ennobled women into powerless objects – pure and unproductive.

Except that they controlled the ultimate and most life-threatening or -affirming production – that of children. The medical convention was that if a doctor were forced to choose between mother and child, he should save the child. And so the mother made the ultimate sacrifice of powerlessness.

These are all explanations, not justifications. There is every reason to be disappointed. After all, on almost every other subject these two friends were pushing an agenda at least a half a century ahead of the Western norm, if not a century.

IN MANY WAYS not just Baldwin but also LaFontaine seemed happier in Toronto. By September 1849 Baldwin was back in his Front Street house. It would now become the gathering place, as LaFontaine's house had been in Montreal, with one added advantage. Baldwin's children were now back in Toronto from Quebec City.

The prime minister and Adèle arrived in November and took a house on Bay Street, less than a block away from the Baldwins. The two friends could walk the few blocks along the wooden sidewalks of Front Street, passing Bishop Strachan's Palace, before arriving at the long, cream stone, neoclassical legislature. Steps ran along the full facade of the central block, leading up to the porch. But a quarter-century after its inauguration, there was still no columned portico. From that uncovered porch you could gaze across the formal gardens to Toronto Bay, before going in through the doors to the main hall, with the Legislative Council on the left and the Legislative Assembly on the right.

Alternatively, they could ride in either's carriage or sleigh up Bay and west along King, past the Governor General's mansion on the left, to the old Toronto Hospital just across John Street. It had been converted into government head-quarters.

LaFontaine and Adèle were not social beings. They had their informal family living half a block away. During those two years in Toronto, Baldwin's daughter Eliza married a rising young man, John Ross, in a grand marriage. His son Robert got his wish and went off to sea. His mother, Phoebe, died aged eighty, the end of a generation.

There were dinners with the judges and senior lawyers in Osgoode Hall, William Warren's building. The long table is still there in the big dining room, with portraits of the two Reformers hanging over it. This was a safe, comfortable world they both understood.

When there was a parliamentary break the two families often took the boat down Lake Ontario to Niagara-on-the-

Lake and from there went overland to Niagara Falls. It was then still a reasonably wild spot with a comfortable wooden hotel built on the edge of the chasm and a dramatic open porch. People went there for their health, to relax. Cabinet meetings were held there.

The atmosphere in Toronto rapidly became very welcoming. The crisis was past. Torontonians, only a year before so divided across religious and political lines, began to enjoy the cultural complexity involved in being the Canadian capital.

The Elgins by now also felt that they had come through the fire and survived. Having given up political power, he was busy inventing the modern Governor General, the effective head of state and a symbol of unity above politics. With his wife, he originated the idea of the vice-regal couple as supporters of culture. They were everywhere, constantly travelling, meeting people, entertaining, backing cultural initiatives. There was now an interesting, close relationship between the two Reformers and Elgin, although LaFontaine tended to complain privately about having to be present at official evenings until one or two in the morning.

Bit by bit LaFontaine and Baldwin were wearing down. We cannot now imagine how power then worked – the thousands of handwritten letters from each of them going in every direction, replacing what we now do by phone or email or fax or face-to-face conversation; drafting hundreds of bills, guiding them through Parliament; sitting on the front bench day after day, night after night five to six months of the year trying to lead an increasingly fractious party.

On January 10, 1850, Baldwin collapsed. It was on the eve of the anniversary of Eliza's death and thus the darkest moment of his year. His deep mourning may have unleashed the effects of his terrible fatigue. LaFontaine felt that he was better on the twelfth; two weeks later he was worrying about his friend's going back to work too soon. In February LaFontaine began plotting to send Baldwin off to New York on a holiday. "Otherwise I fear that he will be seriously weakened." A month later Baldwin's gaiety seemed to have returned, then "yesterday he once again had head pains" – a sort of shaking disturbance inside – "he stays home, this morning, he is better, the pain gone; this afternoon the pain is back, he suffers badly; at four o'clock Leslie and I went to see him; he made an effort to be gay, but admits he suffers. As we left, he shook our hands and burst into tears." He won't go away, won't leave his family. "I am going to try something else, take all his papers and force him, against his wishes, to do nothing." But LaFontaine was doing little better himself. "I don't know how I hold up. The weight increases every day and every day is heavier."

Young though they still were, they became like a strange old couple, fussing about each other's decline. By the middle of the year LaFontaine began to talk of resigning. "I haven't been well for a good while. The fact is I am almost exhausted." His inflammatory rheumatism started creeping back. By early 1851 he was in its grip and could not sleep. He was relieved that Baldwin had recovered enough to act for them both in the House. And he was happy when the winter was cold enough to get out with Adèle in their sleigh.

THE REFORM PARTY, undisciplined by a weak Opposition, was slowly breaking into four factions, the Clear Grits being the most troublesome. They felt, as Papineau did at the other extreme, that the Reformers were too careful, too compromising. They, like Papineau, were addicted to European belief systems focused on the sort of clarity that would bring conflict to Canada.

After the general amnesty of 1849 William Lyon Mackenzie moved back to Toronto. In early 1851 he was elected in a by-election. On Thursday, June 26, he moved a motion to investigate the Court of Chancery, which Baldwin had gone to a lot of trouble to reform only two years before.

It was a nuisance motion, the sort of thing Mackenzie had always specialized in. But it was defeated that evening by only four votes, because most Upper Canadian MPs had voted alongside Mackenzie and the Clear Grits, a sign of internal party rumbling.

Baldwin simply resigned. LaFontaine, Hincks, those who had sided with Mackenzie only a few hours before all tried to dissuade him. But he had had enough. On Monday, June 30, with LaFontaine beside him on the front bench, he got up in the House. After dealing with the court question, he began to talk about his own career in public life, his *humble talents*. He talked of his friends, who had made this great experiment in democracy possible, of their *zealous and disinterested patriotism which has never been exceeded*. He was then overcome and began weeping, but continued on for a few minutes to thank in particular *my friends in Lower Canada. I will never forget the noble and generous confidence they have bestowed upon me*. As he sat down, all those around him were crying.

LaFontaine refused to replace Baldwin. Instead, he announced his own retirement at the end of the session.

On October 1 he was feted at a great banquet in Montreal. Wolfred Nelson, offering thanks, called him "le Cincinnatus du Canada." LaFontaine's speech that night was constructed as if it were the conclusion to his "Address to the Electors of Terrebonne" eleven years before. The central theme in both was egalitarianism. Yes, he was retiring, but *le pouvoir est aujourd'hui entre les mains du peuple. Power today is in the people's hands.*

A few days later LaFontaine left office. He was forty-four. Baldwin was forty-seven.

CHAPTER TEN

Not Quietly Toward the End

And that was that. They simply walked away.

It is true that neither of them enjoyed politics. LaFontaine had always been obsessive about the conditions in which he accepted power. And Baldwin had a history of resigning whenever power got in the way of ethics. But you could hardly call them quitters. They had persisted long enough to accomplish something thought impossible. Yet they weren't men for deep chairs and strong drink and backrooms and endless plotting. As time went on, they increasingly let slip into their letters that they found the requirements of politics disgusting. Yet they were not priggish or brittle or puritan. And over a dozen years they had shown themselves to be better at politics than any of those who were *naturals* or enjoyed its rough-and-tumble or took pleasure in the trading and debating. After all, Baldwin had been brought up in politics, and LaFontaine had been at the centre of great political dramas even before leaving school. Perhaps what set them apart was what John Sanfield Macdonald said of Baldwin – a "pure love of justice and the unaffected honesty of his character." Unlike most men in politics, they did not see it as being about themselves.

Perhaps most important they did not leave office for political reasons. They were not losing power. Their majority was perfectly workable. Lower Canada was solid. The Upper Canadian fracture was reparable. William Lyon Mackenzie would have been easy to isolate, just as Papineau had been. The Clear Grits were not the natural inheritors of the Reform movement. As time would show, even with every lucky break, they could not bring the Liberal Party to power in any sustainable way. Why? Because the Clear Grits represented an imported view of politics unrelated to Canadian realities.

The Liberal Party as an organism capable of winning and holding power would not come into existence until forty years later, when Wilfrid Laurier cleansed it of this Grit sectarianism. In the meantime the original Reform movement would continually mutate, with Morin and Hincks taking over from LaFontaine and Baldwin, the emphasis shifting to the resolution of the seigneurie problem and to the building of railways. Then the Compact/Tories/Conservatives abandoned their old positions so that MacNab could take power with Morin, incredibly, on the basis of a Reform program. The cynic could say that the Reform movement had become more conservative. But it could equally be argued that Reform principles had become the mainstream. They were succeeded by MacNab and Taché – the colonel and doctor who had probably shot William Mason during the attack on LaFontaine's house. He was a red Tory, thus the MacNab–Taché ministry could be called Canada's first red Tory government. Then came Taché and Macdonald; then Macdonald–Cartier, then Cartier–Macdonald, then Confederation, and the long-term direction of the country was set. At the heart of all these mutations – whether driven by narrow ambition or large ideas – was the basic message shaped by LaFontaine and Baldwin: ethics is about programs that bring people together; ideology is divisive; complexity is a strength. In other words, LaFontaine and Baldwin were the fathers of both the modern Liberal Party and the modern Progressive Conservative Party. From time to time the Liberals slip back into the Grit desire for clarity, and the Conservatives slip back into Toryism or even Compacting. For that matter, at its most interesting the CCF/NDP has owed much more to the LaFontaine–Baldwin idea of inclusive egalitarianism governed by restraint than the old

European idea of class struggle. And the women's movement, shaped by Nellie McClung and others around the principle of fairness, equally comes out of the Great Ministry's Reform tradition.

AFTER THE SUCCESS of 1848–49, LaFontaine and Baldwin had defined the mainstream. They could therefore easily have sliced off the Clear Grit infection in 1851 and brought in new moderates, people who were beginning to understand what indigenous national policies could look like. They could have stayed in power for a decade. They were young men.

Instead they walked away. It is difficult for us to understand the depth of psychic and physical exhaustion they experienced, in part because we have treated Responsible Government and the creation of a relationship between francophones and anglophones and growing independence from Britain as mere case studies of historic inevitability. We read history backwards. We are here, so what leads to us *had* to happen.

This is not the case. The racial, religious and linguistic wars that dominated Europe and the United States through the seventeenth, eighteenth and nineteenth centuries and the first half of the twentieth century tell us that there was no inevitable destiny at work here. And the general absence of either democracy or stable democracy throughout the West until the second half of the twentieth century – to say nothing of its absence in most colonies and ex-colonies of the European and U.S. empires – tell us that we were not destined for our middle-class, stable, independent parliamentary federalism, certainly not as early as the mid-nineteenth century. And finally, as I cannot help but repeat, there was no movement or desire or goodwill in England that would lead to an independent, democratic Canada, let alone independence or democracy in any other part of the empire. Which is why that democratic and independence process elsewhere in the British and other empires following on the success of Responsible Government in Canada was so drawn out, so painful and often so violent.

Over the past century and a half we have thought of LaFontaine and Baldwin as colonial figures in a distant past very unlike today, men who won out over the local compacts, a handful of uncooperative British governors and some distracted British cabinet ministers. Apart from the narrowly defined concept of government responsibility, no other ideas are thought to have been at play. And the responsibility in question is always presented as little more than a tried-and-true British idea.

All of this is entirely or in good part untrue. Something original and almost impossible was taking place. These two men took on the core beliefs of the most powerful empire of the day and in many ways the most powerful empire to have existed since Rome. They outmanoeuvred it with ideas and language. And the essence of what they accomplished was not Responsible Government. It was the value of moderation when faced with persistent crisis and violence. What's more, unlike most men in politics, they were willing to suffer personal humiliation in order to avoid the use of violence. From the point of view of political philosophy, it was a revolutionary innovation.

They had every reason by 1851 to be voided of psychic and physical energy. If there was one other unexpected element, it was the appearance of a Governor General, Elgin, who somehow understood what was in play and acted as a willing third party in the revolution.

LAFONTAINE WAS NO SOONER BACK in private life in Montreal than he was writing to Baldwin, "I am recovering my health, people say, just as fast as you did yourself after your resignation." In fact, neither of them recovered. There was of course some superficial healing. In the 1840s Baldwin had written of the relief he felt each time he returned to "home – my own dear, dear home … which brings tears into my eyes whenever I think of it." Now it was hard to get him out of his two houses, except perhaps to go to Osgoode Hall, where he could pretend he was above all a legal figure. Already in late 1851 he was writing to John Ross, his son-in-law, about "the relief from mental anxiety which I have experienced since relieved from the responsibilities of office."

Yet he continued to suffer. Almost every day his head rumbled with noise, headaches, giddiness, leaving him confused. He didn't want to show this weakness and so cut himself off from society. LaFontaine was so concerned that he peppered him with telegram inquiries. Finally in March 1852 Baldwin managed a reply. His friend answered back quickly with his sharp tongue: "You are still alive and I am happy. As my last letter went without reply for months I eventually feared that you were no longer of this world." Again the next year he was too sick to go out or to write.

With all of these vicissitudes, Baldwin seemed to lose his senses, running in the December 1851 election for no particular reason, without bothering to campaign. LaFontaine wrote to tell him he was lucky to have lost. In 1852 the University of Toronto tried to persuade him to become chancellor. He was outraged by the reintroduction of some religious influence and so refused. And indeed the Anglicans, Methodists and Catholics were pushing their way back in through their individually affiliated colleges.

LaFontaine seemed more comfortable in his new private life. In 1853 he became chief justice of Lower Canada and chaired the commission that oversaw the ending of the seigneurial system. And he tried to coax Baldwin to travel with Adèle and himself to England and France on a relaxed holiday. Baldwin admitted that his family wanted him to go, but in truth he was worried about dying away from home, away from his cult of Eliza. Freed from public life he had been able to slip back into his old focus on this, his unquenched love.

Then John A. Macdonald, attorney general, attempted to persuade Baldwin to become chief justice of Upper Canada. That way both fathers of our democracy would be overseeing the justice system they had largely defined. He refused.

By 1855 his heart had begun to fail, and on December 9 he died, surrounded by his family. He was fifty-four years old. The city and the province prepared for its first state funeral. Shops shut down. A thousand people walked or rode in the procession, led by the judiciary, the clergy, the politicians, from the new St. James Cathedral all the way to the family's mausoleum at Spadina. His little granddaughter remembered being dressed in black silk with crepe and weeping with the rest.

Before his death, Robert Baldwin had carefully prepared his reunion with Eliza. He was no sooner dead than Maria received a personal memorandum of instructions. With it was a package of the love letters between her mother and father. There was a second package of the letters copied out by Baldwin himself. The copies were for his children – "a memorial of what your parents were to each other ... they are the records of a mutual affection the most deep and of a mutual confidence the most unbounded." Since her death, he explained, these letters had been the source of his continuing conversation with Eliza. He had carried some of them with him everywhere to read at any moment. He had, in that way, never been without her.

Now his memorandum instructed Maria on precisely how he was to be buried:

> [B]efore I am committed to my coffin let the following operation be performed on my body, being the same performed on that of your dear mother – let an incision be made into the cavity of the abdomen extending through the two upper thirds of the linea alba. Secondly, let my little pear

brooch, a present from herself, be placed in my bosom, that as she rests with nuptial ring upon her finger, I may rest beside her with this token of her affection on my breast. Thirdly ... the handkerchief that covered her face while she lay as a corpse prior to her burial, let the same be used to cover mine. Fourthly the chairs on which rested her coffin ... let the same be used to support my coffin; fifthly let the [original] letters be [placed] on my breast near my heart; and let one of my E's handkerchiefs be spread over them.

Finally, he asked that his "coffin be placed by the side of my E's ... the side she used to call her *own*, as nearest my heart, and let a small iron chain be passed round the two coffins and locked so as to chain them together."

All of this Maria made happen, except the operation. That instruction she kept to herself. One month after the funeral, Baldwin's eldest son, Willcocks, found a note from his father on heavy animal-skin parchment folded into four. This note he had carried in his waistcoat pocket every day for years, in case he died away from home. On it he repeated his instructions and implored that if buried without the operation being done, for whatever reason, he should be disinterred. "I earnestly entreat of those who may be about me when I die … that for the love of God, as an act of Christian charity, and by solemn recollection that they may one day have themselves a dying request to make to others, they will not in any account whatever permit my being enclosed in my coffin before the performance of this last solemn injunction."

Immediately his son gathered together with Baldwin's brother-in-law, Lawrence Heydon, and a Dr. Richardson, and went out to the mausoleum.

I have stared at the careful writing on the parchment, as clear and unfaded as if written yesterday instead of 170 years ago. I have thought of those three men going into the mausoleum in the cold of mid-winter, unlocking the chain, lifting the lid of his casket, carefully moving all of Eliza's objects, parting his clothes in order to cut him open in the manner of a Caesarean. And I have thought about the implications of his instructions. Strange, yes. Obsessive, somewhat overwrought, yes.

But why reduce the last act of what was the most remarkable love story of Canadian public life to Freudian analysis? We know that he loved her to distraction. He loved no other woman. He never got over her. After they first met and she was sent away from him to New York, he wrote, "You do not know My beloved Eliza how interwoven you are I might almost say with my being." That love was his anchor in the life of public service that he felt obliged to live because of his sense of duty. Those are facts. Why should such love in a great public man not be taken for what it was?

LaFontaine lived on for another five years. He took great pleasure in working with a small group on research for the Société Historique de Montréal. For example, he wrote a fascinating fifty-page analysis of the slavery officially encouraged in New France, an unexpected continuation of his long-standing opposition to the slave trade. In 1859 Adèle, who had been sick for years, finally died. She was forty-six. He seemed to accept this loss of his closest friend of twenty-six years almost as a release for her.

TWO YEARS LATER he remarried a distant relative – a widow with three young daughters. Suddenly, at fifty-four years old, he was thrown into the family life he had always desired, and it brought him great pleasure. A year later, his wife, Jane, bore him the son he had always dreamt of, named for himself. In 1864 she was pregnant again. Neither child survived long, but he would not know this. In one of his last letters to a newer friend: "My son is by my side and seems to be saying that for over a month now he has been two years old."

In February 1864 he was struck by an apoplectic attack in his office of chief justice. He was rushed home in time to take his son in his arms before slipping into a coma, then dying. He was fifty-six years old.

He was treated in those last hours by Dr. Horace Henry Nelson, who was almost certainly the son LaFontaine had offered to adopt a quarter-century before when Wolfred Nelson was sent into exile.

Like Baldwin's in Toronto, his was the largest funeral Montreal had ever seen, with twelve thousand people. Notre Dame was jammed, large parts of the city were closed, and thousands followed his casket to the cemetery on Mount Royal.

Two friends had died. A country would be built in the image of their idea.

Works by Louis-Hippolyte LaFontaine

De la famille des Lauson. Vice-rois et lieutenants généraux des rois de France en Amérique. Montréal, 1859.

De l'esclavage en Canada. Montréal, 1859.

Les deux girouettes, ou l'hypocrisie démasquée. Montréal, 1834.

Notes sur l'inamovibilité des curés dans le Bas-Canada. Montréal, 1837.

Parliamentary Debates

Canadian Mirror of Parliament. G. Beaumont, ed. Kingston: Chronicle and Gazette Office, 1841. (Reports of debates of the Legislative Assembly of United Canada for the year 1841 collected from various newspapers.)

Debates of the Legislative Assembly of United Canada, 1841–1867. Montréal: Presses de L'école des hautes études commerciales, 1970–1994. (Reconstructed debates of the Legislative Assembly of United Canada from newspaper and other sources.)

Journals of the Legislative Assembly of the Province of Canada.
Journals of the Legislative Council of the Province of Canada.

Hansard, 1803–2005. London: Parliament of the United Kingdom, 1803–2005. (Hansard of the House of Commons of the United Kingdom. A useful source for significant debates in the 1840s about Responsible Government in Canada.)

Mirror of Parliament of the Province of Canada. Montreal: M. Reynolds, 1846. (Reports of debates of the Legislative Assembly of United Canada for the year 1846 collected from various newspapers.)

Published Collections

The Durham Papers. Sessional Paper No. 23.

Baldwin, Robert. "To the Free and Independent Electors of the County of Rimouski." *The Globe*, October 1, 1844.

———. "Address to Electors of the North Riding of York." *The Globe*, October 1, 1843.

Doughty, Sir Arthur. *The Elgin–Grey Papers, 1846–1852.* 4 vols. Ottawa, 1937.

Hincks, Francis. *Reminiscences of His Public Life.* Montreal: William Drysdale, 1884.

Howe, Joseph. *The Speeches and Public Letters of Joseph Howe.* Halifax: The Chronicle Publishing Company, 1909.

LaFontaine, Louis-Hippolyte. *Journal de voyage en Europe: 1837–1838.* Québec: Septentrion, 1999.

———. *Au nom de la loi: Lettres de Louis-Hippolyte LaFontaine à divers correspondants, 1829–1847.* Montréal: Éditions Varia, 2002.

———. *Les ficelles de pouvoir: Correspondence entre Louis-Hippolyte LaFontaine et Robert Baldwin, 1840–1854.* Montréal: Éditions Varia, 2002.

Nelson, Wolfred. *Écrits d'un Patriote: 1812–1842.* Montréal: Georges Aubin, 1998.

————. *Wolfred Nelson et Son Temps*. Montréal: Éditions de Flambeau, 1946.

Papineau, Louis-Joseph, and Wolfred Nelson. *Résumé impartial de la discussion Papineau–Nelson sur les événements de Saint-Denis en 1837*. Montréal: 1848.

Stewart, Yolande, ed. *My Dear Friend: Letters of Louis-Hippolyte LaFontaine and Robert Baldwin*. Toronto: Plum Hollow Books, 1978.

Early Canadian Newspapers

L'Avenir. (1847.) (A Liberal newspaper known for its support of Responsible Government.)

The Globe. (1844–1858.) (Published by LaFontaine–Baldwin ally George Brown, this was an important venue for the promotion of the Reform position.)

La Minèrve. (1826–1837, 1842–1899.) (Originally published by Auguste-Norbert Morin as a mouthpiece for Louis-Joseph Papineau's Parti patriote, in its second incarnation it became an important French-language supporter of Responsible Government and the Reform position.)

The Montreal Pilot. (1844–1851.) (Published by LaFontaine–Baldwin ally Francis Hincks, this newspaper supported the Reform position throughout this period.)

The Gazette. (1841–1858.) (Montreal's major English-language newspaper. Largely opposed to the Reform platform and inimical to LaFontaine and Baldwin.)

The Toronto Examiner. (1840–1851). (Originally established by Francis Hincks, this newspaper was largely supportive of the

Reform platform. It gradually declined with the success of *The Globe*.)

Biographical Works about LaFontaine and Baldwin

Baldwin, Lawrence. "The Baldwin Legacy, 1799–1999." Private pamphlet.

Baldwin, R.M. and J. *The Baldwins and the Great Experiment*. Toronto: Longmans, 1969.

Bertrand, Réal. *Louis-Hippolyte LaFontaine*, Montréal: Lidec, 1993.

Bruneau, M.A.A. "LaFontaine et Laurier." Discours donné devant le club Libéral de la partie est de Montréal, le 17 avril 1901.

Careless, J.M.S. *Robert Baldwin: The Pre-Confederation Premiers: Ontario Government Leaders, 1841–1867*. Toronto: University of Toronto Press, 1980.

Cross, M.S., and R.L. Frazier. *The Waste That Lies before Me: The Public and Private Worlds of Robert Baldwin*. Canadian Historical Association, Historical Papers. 1983.

Cross, Michael, and Robert Frazier. "Robert Baldwin." *Dictionary of Canadian Biography*. Toronto and Montreal: University of Toronto and Université Laval, 1966–2005.

De Celles, Alfred D. *LaFontaine et son temps*. Montréal: Librairie Beauchemin, 1909.

Jones, Mary J. "Memories of My Youth and a Sketch of the Family History of the Ross–Baldwin Families by Their Descendent" (unpublished).

Leacock, Stephen. *Baldwin, LaFontaine, Hincks: Responsible Government*. Toronto: Morag, 1907.

Monet, Jacques. "Louis-Hippolyte LaFontaine." *Dictionary of Canadian Biography*. Toronto and Montreal: University of Toronto and Université Laval, 1966–2005.

"Some Account of the Settlement in Canada of Robert Baldwin, 'The Emigrant.'" By a granddaughter.

Wilson, George. *The Life of Robert Baldwin: A Study in the Struggle for Responsible Government*. Toronto: The Ryerson Press, 1933.

Hommages à LaFontaine. Montréal: Le Comité du Monument LaFontaine, 1931.

Biographies of LaFontaine and Baldwin Contemporaries

Beck, J. Murray. *Joseph Howe: Conservative Reformer*. Kingston and Montreal: McGill–Queen's University Press, 1982.

Beer, Donald R. *Sir Allan Napier MacNab*. Hamilton, ON: Ontario Heritage Foundation, 1984.

Boyd, John. *Sir George-Étienne Cartier, Baronet: Sa vie et son temps*. Montréal: Librairie Beauchemin, 1918.

Cahill, Barry. "R. v. Howe (1835) for Seditious Libel: A Tale of Twelve Magistrates." *Canadian State Trials*, Vol. 1, ed. Greenwood and Wright (1996).

Godfrey, Charles. *John Rolph: Rebel with Causes*. Madoc, ON: Codam, 1994.

Kilbourn, William. *The Firebrand: William Lyon Mackenzie and the Rebellion of Upper Canada*. Toronto: Clarke, Irwin and Company, 1956.

Schull, Joseph. *Edward Blake: The Man of the Other Way, 1833–1881*. Toronto: Macmillan, 1975.

Sweeny, Alastair. *George-Étienne Cartier: A Biography*. Toronto: McClelland & Stewart, 1976.

General Works

Toronto's Classic Centennial Story: St. Lawrence Hall. Toronto, 1967.

Burn, D.L. "Canada and the Repeal of the Corn Laws." *Cambridge Historical Journal* 2, no. 3 (1928): 252–72.

Cooke, William, ed. *The Parish and Cathedral of St. James, 1797–1997: A Collaborative History*. Toronto: University of Toronto Press, 1998.

David, L-O. *L'Union des Deux Canadas: 1841–1867*. Montréal: Sénécal, 1898.

Davin, Nicholas Flood. *Irishman in Canada*. Toronto: Maclear and Company, 1877.

Deschenes, Gaston. *Un capital éphémère*. Sillery: Les Cahiers du Septentrios, 1999.

Friedland, Martin. *The University of Toronto: A History*. Toronto: University of Toronto Press, 2002.

Leacock, Stephen. "Responsible Government in the British Colonial System." *The American Political Science Review* 1, no. 3 (May 1907): 355–92.

Lefroy, Catherine F. *Recollections of May Warren Breckenridge*. Ontario Historical Society, 1901.

Martin, Chester. *Empire and Commonwealth: Studies in Governance and Self-Government in Canada*. Oxford: Clarendon, 1929.

McGowan, Mark G. *Death or Canada: The Irish Famine Migration to Toronto, 1847*. Toronto: Novalis, 2009.

Monet, Jacques. *The Last Cannon Shot: A Study of French Canadian Nationalism, 1837–1850*. Toronto: University of Toronto Press, 1969.

Ormsby, W.G. *The Emergence of the Federal Concept in Canada, 1839–1845*. Toronto: University of Toronto Press, 1969.

Pinals, Roberts. "Theodore Roosevelt's Inflammatory Rheumatism." *Journal of Clinical Rheumatology* 14, no. 1 (February 2008): 41–44.

Roy, Alain. "Le Marché Sainte-Anne, le Parlement de Montréal et la formation d'un état moderne." Rapport présenté à l'Institut d'histoire de l'Amérique française. Montréal.

Schrauwers, Albert. *Awaiting the Millennium: The Children of Peace and the Village of Hope, 1812–1889*. Toronto: University of Toronto Press, 1993.

Siedle, F. Leslie, and Louis Massicotte. *Taking Stock of 150 Years of Responsible Government in Canada*. Ottawa: The Canadian Study of Parliament Group, 1998.

Tucker, Gilbert. "The Famine Immigration to Canada, 1847." *The American Historical Review* 36, no. 3 (April 1931): 533–49.

Tupper, Sir Charles. *Recollections of Sixty Years in Canada*. Toronto: Cassell and Co., 1914.

Dictionary of Canadian Biography. Toronto and Montreal: University of Toronto and Université Laval, 1966–2005. (Useful as a source of biographies of major Canadian political and social figures during this period.)

Oxford Dictionary of National Biography. Oxford: Oxford University Press, 2004–10. (Useful as a source of biographies of major British political and social figures during this period.)

ACKNOWLEDGMENTS

In the public, indeed the private, world of the mid-nineteenth century, almost everything was written down. The Victorian middle-class mindset of privacy and discretion was not yet in place. There are tens of thousands of letters by and related to LaFontaine and Baldwin, often of a still-vibrant candour, to say nothing of the multitudes of documents of all sorts and many newspapers of small circulation but bold beliefs.

How exciting it is to hold these letters in your hands and think about the circumstances in which they were written. The largest collection of Baldwin's papers is at the Toronto Reference Library in the Baldwin Room, where Mary Rae Shantz and Bill Hamade were extremely helpful. Michael Cross very generously allowed me to read his unpublished biography of Baldwin, which HE MUST FINISH AND PUBLISH. David Baldwin, in an amazing gesture, handed over to me two steamer trunks of papers, which are now added to the Baldwin Room collection. Patricia Kennedy at the Library and Archives Canada was yet again a great guide, as were Nancy Mallett and others at the archives of St. James Cathedral in Toronto, Steve Mackinnon and Patrick

Cummins at the City of Toronto Archives, and David Bogart at the Ontario Legislature.

In Montreal, Jean-René Lassonde at the Bibliothèque Nationale du Québec was wonderfully imaginative. Claude Pronovost at the Marché Bonsecours helped, with his passion for this history, as did Marc Lacasse at the Sulpiciens; Dinu Bumbaru at Héritage Montréal; the archivists at the Ville de Montréal who hold a part of LaFontaine's papers attached to the papers of the Société Historique de Montréal. And Eric Bédard with his new book, *Les Réformistes*, is an inspiration.

Lord and Lady Elgin have been a constant help over the past decade. The enormous collection of letters, scrapbooks, documents and objects belonging to his great-grandfather is now in Ottawa at the Library and Archives Canada, thanks to his efforts and to those of Ian Wilson, the former national archivist. Regarding his devotion to the collection, Andrew Bruce, the 11th Earl of Elgin, has been remarkable, and it should be said that his family is the only one of the British Governors General to have kept up their Canadian link, perhaps because his great-grandfather was the only one to overcome the limits of colonial power and make a decisive contribution to Canada, a contribution that went well beyond his brief term of office here.

Finding and making my way through all of this original material was possible only thanks to the originality and intellectual energy of Thomas Hodd and Jon Weier. Thomas has also been a great help on the whole Extraordinary Canadians series. As for Adrienne, the one constant commentator over the years on my LaFontaine–Baldwin ideas, love and thanks as always flow.

Finally, writing this book and editing this series have been great pleasures, and it has all worked thanks to the support of David Davidar, Diane Turbide, Mary Opper and everyone at Penguin, as well as the seventeen other writers.

1790–1804	LaFontaine's grandfather elected to the Assembly of Lower Canada.
1799	The Baldwins arrive in Upper Canada.
1804	May 12: Robert Baldwin born at home in York (Toronto).
1807	October 4: Louis-Hippolyte LaFontaine born in a wood farmhouse in Boucherville.
1813	April 27: U.S. forces attack York; William Warren Baldwin serves as a battlefield doctor; Robert Baldwin flees with the rest of the family.
	July: U.S. forces take York again.
1815	Louis-Joseph Papineau elected Speaker of the Lower Canada Assembly.
1820	William Warren Baldwin first elected to Upper Canada legislature.
1820–24	LaFontaine at Le Petit Séminaire in Montreal.
1824	Election of first Upper Canada Assembly; majority critical of Compact government.

1825	Baldwin falls in love with Eliza Sullivan.
	June 20: Baldwin called to the bar.
1827	Archdeacon John Strachan negotiates the gift of 226,000 acres of public land to the Anglican Church, creating the clergy reserve problem.
	May 31: Baldwin and Eliza married.
1829	August 18: LaFontaine called to the bar.
1830	Upper Canada Reformers lose majority.
	October 26: LaFontaine elected for Terrebonne.
1831	Sharon Temple built.
	July 9: LaFontaine marries Adèle Berthelot.
1834	William Lyon Mackenzie becomes the first elected mayor of Toronto.
	February 21: 92 Resolutions voted by the Lower Canada Assembly.
1835	March 2: Joseph Howe libel trial; he is acquitted.
1836	January 11: Eliza dies after almost two years of agony brought on by a Caesarean birth.

February–April: Baldwin briefly joins government.

April 30: Baldwin goes to London and Cork for several months.

1837 October–November: Lower Canada Rebellion.

November 24: Wolfred Nelson and George-Étienne Cartier defeat the British in the Battle of Saint-Denis; Louis-Joseph Papineau flees to the United States.

December: Upper Canada Rebellion.

December 5: Baldwin acts as middleman between rebels and the governor; battle at Yonge and Maitland.

December 26: LaFontaine crosses the border to the U.S. and sails to England.

1838 February 26: LaFontaine flees London to Paris.

April 1838–February 1841: Martial law in Lower Canada.

May 28: Lord Durham arrives as Governor General.

June 22: LaFontaine back in Montreal.

November 4: LaFontaine is arrested.

December 13: LaFontaine is released.

1839   John Strachan becomes first Anglican bishop
of Toronto.

February 4: Lord Durham's report is
presented to the Colonial Office.

April 12: Francis Hincks writes LaFontaine to
propose an alliance between Lower and Upper
Canadian Reformers.

April 21: LaFontaine replies.

November 11: Durham leaves.

1840   August 25: LaFontaine publishes his "Adresse
aux électeurs de Terrebonne."

September 16: Hincks translates and
publishes the "Address" in English in his
Toronto paper, *The Examiner.*

November 26: Baldwin writes to LaFontaine.

1841   June 14: First Session of the United Canadas
Parliament in Kingston.

August: Governor General sends violent gangs to Terrebonne; LaFontaine withdraws from election.

August 21: Baldwin's alternative riding, North York, invites LaFontaine to run.

September 3: Baldwin introduces Responsible Government resolutions in Parliament.

September 21: LaFontaine elected.

1842   LaFontaine and Baldwin elected vice-presidents of International Anti-Slavery Society.

January 10: Sir Charles Bagot arrives as new Governor General.

September 26: LaFontaine and Baldwin named to government.

1843   Election Reform Bill; Baldwin elected in Rimouski; England passes Canada's Corn Act.

March: Lord Metcalfe replaces the dying Bagot as Governor General.

November 24: LaFontaine and Baldwin resign.

1844	March: Creation of the Reform Association.
	November 4: LaFontaine's adopted daughter, Corinne, dies.
	November 12: Election defeat for Reformers.
1845	Wolfred Nelson elected; Papineau returns.
	January 31: Law re-establishing role of French passed.
1846	June 26: U.K. repeals Corn Laws.
1847	January 30: Lord Elgin sworn in.
	May–October: 90,000 Irish immigrants arrive.
1848	January 28: Election: LaFontaine and Baldwin win clear majority.
	February 2: Joseph Howe and James Uniake take over in Nova Scotia.
	March 11: LaFontaine government sworn in.
	August 14: U.K. gives in and repeals English-only clause in Canadian constitution.
1849	General pardon of the remaining exiled rebels; William Lyon Mackenzie returns.

Baldwin's Municipal Corporations Act (the Baldwin Act) creates municipal democracy; abolition of imprisonment for debt; limiting of range of appeals to U.K. Privy Council; new legal appeal system plus decentralizing of courts.

February 14: Rebellion Losses Bill introduced.

March 9: Rebellion Losses Bill passed.

April 25: Elgin signs Rebellion Losses Bill; mob burns down Parliament.

April 26: MPs meet in upstairs ballroom of the Bonsecours Market; LaFontaine's house is sacked.

April 30: Elgin almost killed going to Château Ramezay to receive Address of Loyalty from the legislature.

May 9: Visiting Upper Canadian Reform delegation is attacked by mob.

May 30: Reform of Law Courts.

August 15: Second violent attack on LaFontaine's house—one attacker shot dead.

August 20: Assassination attempt on
LaFontaine at coroner's inquiry.

September 10: Annexation Manifesto signed
by Montreal Anglo anti-democracy merchants
and French-Canadian nationalists; Cartier
organizes an Anti-Annexation Manifesto.

November 14: Toronto declared the new capital of Canada to alternate with Quebec City.

December 13: George Brown launches Clear
Grit movement.

1849–50   The University of Toronto Act – Baldwin
creates the basis of the Canadian public
university system.

1850   January 10: Baldwin suffers an emotional
breakdown, which continues off and on
through spring.

1851   William Lyon Mackenzie is elected in a
by-election.

January 1: Primogeniture is abolished.

February 22: Authority over postal system is
transferred from London; creation of uniform
low postal rates.

June 30: Baldwin resigns.

September 22: Canadian capital moves to Quebec City.

September 26: LaFontaine resigns.

1852   November: Baldwin refuses chancellorship of the University of Toronto.

1853   August 13: LaFontaine named chief justice of Lower Canada; becomes first French-Canadian baronet and named papal knight by Pope.

1854   Elgin negotiates Reciprocity Treaty between Canada and the U.S.; Baldwin refuses John A. Macdonald's invitation to become chief justice of Upper Canada.

        November 23: Seigneurial system is abolished; clergy reserves are secularized.

1855   March 15: Governor General becomes commander-in-chief; LaFontaine named president of the tribunal to wind up the seigneurial system.

1858   January 1: Dollar becomes official monetary unit of Canada.

July 28: Macdonald–Cartier government falls when Parliament refuses Ottawa as Canada's permanent capital.

August 1: Cartier–Macdonald government persuades Parliament to choose Ottawa as the permanent capital.

December 9: Baldwin dies, aged fifty-four.

1859   January: Baldwin's tomb reopened to perform "Caesarean" operation.

May 27: Lady LaFontaine dies, aged fifty.

November 20: Sod-turning for Parliament Buildings in Ottawa.

1860   July 1: Native People's affairs transferred from London to Ottawa.

1861   January 30: LaFontaine marries Jane Morrison, a thirty-nine-year-old widow with three young daughters.

August: William Lyon Mackenzie dies.

1862   July 1: LaFontaine's first son, Louis-Hippolyte, is born.

1863   *Les Anciens Canadiens* by Philippe Aubert de Gaspé is published.

1864	February 26: LaFontaine dies, aged fifty-six.
	September 1–9: Charlottetown Conference.
1865	October 10–28: Quebec Conference.
1866–67	December 1866–March 1867: London Conference.
1867	July 1: Confederation.